ood Wardens Development Officer • Street Lighting 1 & 2 • Community
TV Monitoring • Eastserve 1, 2 & 3 • Eastserve Broadband • EMBRACE •
ent Officer • Community Conferencing   hbour
s • School Security • Youth Developme   n Core
n Intervention Officer • Duke of Edinbu   aching
aching & Learning • Social Inclusion a   Action
nd Curriculum Enrichment • Managem   ational
Raising Attainment and Standards • Key Stage 3 & 4 Curriculum • Year
ties • Learning for Life • Infrastructure Partnerships and Sustainability
rental Involvement • On Track Roll-Out • Off-Roll Pupils • Full Service
entary Education • Ashbury Meadow Primary School • Pyramid Clubs •
1 & 2 • Student Pathways • East Manchester Academy: City East Library
ools Where Every Child Matters • Medlock Valley Alternative Education •
nwealth Games Pre-Volunteer Programme • Community Environmental
Step Ahead • Skills for Life 1,2,3 & 4 • Preparation for Work • Aspire •
native Curriculum • Local Labour into Construction • Construction Skills
evelopment Package • Company Growth 1 & 2 • Business Support Advice
ation • Growth Through Diversification • Micro Business Support 1 & 2
um Local Purchase and Supply • Property Database • SEEDS • Childcare
s • Employment and Training • Sector Specific Support • Regeneration
Project • Vocational Learning Centre • Job Brokerage • Enhanced Job
port • Whitworth Building Community Learning Centre • Demolitions
ransfer • New Approaches to Social Housing • Stock Transfer: Eastlands
lay • Environmental Programme Management: Projects and Campaigns
ive Open Space 1 & 2 • Positive Open Space: Maintenance • Community
eet Youth Provision • The Grange Community Resource Centre 1 & 2 • NDC
to School • Bradford Park and The Grange • Openshaw Park • Community
Improving Access to Community Buildings • Access to Local Services •
aw Healthy Living Centre • Environmental Support • Managing Areas in
ordinator • Health and Well-Being Development • Family Support Sure
ok • Drugs and Alcohol Education • Healthy Living 1 & 2 • Family Support
sylum Seeker Project • Integrated Adult Services • Social Regeneration
Development • Credit Union 1 & 2 • Financial Inclusion • Environmental
ity Sector • Voluntary and Community Sector Consortium • Increasing
city Building Programme Support • Building Community Capacity 1 & 2
l Capacity Building • Community Reporters • Small Grants Endowment
acons Art and Culture Programme • East Feast • Research and Evaluation
y • Participation in the Beacons Programme • Pride in East Manchester

RECLAIMING EAST MANCHESTER

Ten years of resident-led regeneration

RECLAIMING EAST MANCHESTER

Ten years of resident-led regeneration

Len Grant

Clayton resident Diane Vickers welcomes John Prescott to the Stuart Street community garden, 2004

Inspirational change

Improving the quality of people's lives was one of the most important priorities set by the Labour Government in 1997. In our most deprived neighbourhoods a dramatically new approach was needed to tackle years of under-investment and decline. We listened to other views – residents, planners, academics as well as practitioners – and established New Deal for Communities as a flagship regeneration programme within our broader Neighbourhood Renewal strategy. My colleagues and I were determined that residents would, for the first time, be the decision-makers in bringing about real change.

As this book of achievement demonstrates, the journey in east Manchester has not been without its challenges. Entrenched social problems, particularly around crime, a poor physical environment, low educational attainment, and acute levels of unemployment added together to make east Manchester absolutely the right place to test our new approach.

Only with genuine resident involvement has progress been made and, as many testify here, the neighbourhoods of Beswick, Clayton and Openshaw have truly been transformed beyond all recognition. On my visits to east Manchester – playing football with Tony Blair in the refurbished Bradford Park which we opened in September 2002, or touring a community garden with its own bandstand in Clayton in 2004 – the resolve residents have shown to turn around their estates, their streets, their schools and their back yards, has been inspirational.

Although the statistics show great improvements in crime reduction and exam results, for example, it is local people's renewed commitment to east Manchester, to building a brighter future for themselves and their families, that will sustain future generations.

May I add my congratulations to all the residents and staff who have made the last ten years such a success and invite you all to maintain your commitment as east Manchester continues to reach its potential.

The Right Honourable John Prescott MP
Deputy Prime Minister, 1997–2007

Richard Leese joins in the celebrations after east Manchester wins £25 million SRB funding, 1999

A belief in the future

By the late '90s east Manchester was a real conundrum for Manchester City Council and our partners. Just how do you turn around such a large area of entrenched deprivation?

Barcelona had taught us that an international sporting event could lead to massive urban transformation. Although our bid for the 2000 Olympics was unsuccessful, we learnt important lessons which, in 1995, helped us to secure the 17th Commonwealth Games. A key reason for securing these Games was to use them to kick-start the regeneration of east Manchester.

Our track record of successfully delivering regeneration is good: Hulme and the city centre are rightly held up as examples of best practice. However, the challenge set by east Manchester was much tougher and needed a different approach if we were to succeed. Central to this new approach has been putting residents at the very heart of the regeneration process. They have enthusiastically grasped this opportunity and have been instrumental in ensuring that together, we got it right.

The Games were an outstanding success and were hugely beneficial to the city as a whole and to east Manchester specifically. Their legacy has continued to grow with the 'Blues' returning back to their roots in east Manchester and with ambitious plans to further develop Sportcity.

Not only has east Manchester been a test bed for inclusive resident engagement, but innovative new public services were conceived and tested here before being rolled out across the city and beyond. Much of what we know about dealing with antisocial behaviour, tackling unemployment and improving open space, we've learnt from the Beacons experience. Embedding best practice in the mainstream delivery of services is just one part of the legacy.

I remember celebrating with residents when funding was initially secured and I count myself fortunate to have witnessed the whole ten-year journey since then. I cannot congratulate residents highly enough. The scale of transformation is remarkable. Despair and hopelessness have been replaced by fierce pride and a belief in the future.

But this is not the end. Far from it. We were always clear that east Manchester's renaissance would take at least 30 years to complete. The east Manchester New Deal for Communities programme represents the beginning of the revival and I look forward to continuing to work with residents in the years to come to build on this great start.

Sir Richard Leese
Leader, Manchester City Council

Sean McGonigle and residents celebrate the opening of offices in Beswick Precinct, 1998

The early years

In 1997 I was leading the Council's housing programme in Hulme and Moss Side but, as Hulme's five-year City Challenge programme was coming to an end, I was summoned to the town hall. The Council had just won £18 million from the Estates Renewal Challenge Fund (ERCF) to pay for the transfer of 7,000 council houses in Wythenshawe and, encouraged by their success in the south of the city, the Director of Housing, Steve Mycio, asked if I would help put together an ERCF bid for east Manchester. With some apprehension I accepted and started my new job in the August of that year.

The first place I was shown was the Redvers Street area of Lower Beswick and, even though I had worked in housing for many years, I'd never seen anything like it before. It was scary as hell. There was row upon row of boarded-up properties, with brown metal shuttering over all the doors and windows. Rubbish and burnt-out cars were everywhere. The place was just awful and it left a deep impression on me.

I'd come across some alarming stuff in Hulme and Moss Side but this was very different. There the Council owned most of the property and had responsibility for managing it, not always very successfully. But in Lower Beswick – and other areas like it – it was largely privately owned or run by a housing association. The depths to which east Manchester had sunk were staggering.

The area had huge problems, not just with housing but with crime, lack of jobs, poor environment and education. Towards the end of the 1990s the only government scheme with any significant funds was the ERCF, but that was aimed solely at council house improvements. As well as helping to bid for that larger pot of money, I also supported a smaller bid – in partnership with neighbouring Tameside – in the fourth round of the Single Regeneration Budget (SRB).

Having the support of local people was extremely important in the bidding process but we were faced with some very angry and dissatisfied residents. At one meeting at St Jerome's Church I remember three very vocal women from Higher Openshaw Neighbourhood Association who just took it in turns to stand up and scream at us! At the time we dubbed them the 'Witches of Eastwick' [they were Wendy Eaton, Rita Birch and Elaine Wright] and they were justifiably fed up with a lack of activity in their area. I've got to know them all very well since and we've worked closely over the years. But that meeting was my first experience of local residents' frustration and was a real baptism of fire!

For the ERCF bid we were originally targeting Collyhurst, Beswick, Openshaw, Clayton and Miles Platting. This was not only a large area geographically, but one of the most deprived and challenging in Manchester. Our preliminary bid was for £80 million – much more than Wythenshawe's – but then we did have a huge task ahead of us. Whithall knocked us back, saying our aspirations were too high. They suggested we cut the bid in half to have a better chance. So we chopped out Miles Platting and Collyhurst, submitted a new bid for £42 million and waited. Then, in February, on the day of the decision, and without any warning, we got a phone call to say we hadn't been successful. Apparently the ministers felt they couldn't support our bid because it wasn't a wise investment and wouldn't resolve the problems of east Manchester. We knew that only too well, but what could we do, it was the only funding available.

'...my concern about the ERCF bid which Manchester submitted is that I am not convinced that wholesale transfer and refurbishment of the 3,787 properties on the ten estates in the east Manchester area, as proposed in the bid, is necessarily the right answer nor one that will work in the long-term. Spending money solely on social housing would not deal with the overall housing problems facing east Manchester.

In order to achieve long-term and sustainable regeneration of the east Manchester area and before committing many £millions, we must be sure that any solution is an integrated and comprehensive one which links with Manchester's strategy for dealing with run-down private sector properties...'

Letter from Hilary Armstrong, Minister for Local Government and Housing, to Manchester MP, Tony Lloyd, February 1998.

A few months later, Hilary Armstrong, the Minister for Local Government and Housing, came to east Manchester to explain personally why the ERCF bid had been unsuccessful. We invited all the tenants' association representatives involved in the bidding process to the meeting where she announced that the Government was developing a new approach, something more appropriate for this area. She encouraged us to keep working at bringing people together and to wait for an announcement later that year.

"...then I found out there was going to be a meeting... something about all this money coming into the area. So me and my entourage went flying in. I'll admit, I was very aggressive – never personal – but I'll never apologise for that because it came from my heart and not from my head. I was very, very angry."

Elaine Wright, Openshaw resident.

> "I remember at one of the meetings Hilary Armstrong attended, Maggie Warburton asked her, 'Have you got your cheque book with you?' It was as if Maggie wasn't going to let the minister out until she'd got the money!"
>
> **Rachel Downey, regeneration consultant to Manchester City Council.**

I think it was on that occasion that I first met Maggie Warburton. A feisty Scot, Maggie was the local rep for Clayton and like the 'Witches' she was never reluctant to speak her mind. She collared me at that meeting and challenged me, "I bet you a fiver you won't come along to one of our meetings," she said. "Oh I will," I promised. I did go, and have been to countless meetings like it since, but she never did pay up! (See page 175.) From then on Maggie became hugely involved with the programme and was one of many stalwarts who have made east Manchester's regeneration so successful.

The ERCF was very much a relic of the outgoing Conservative Government and not a relevant solution for many of Britain's regeneration challenges, as we were finding out in east Manchester. The new Labour administration took a fresh look at the problems faced by disadvantaged communities – Tony Blair created the Social Exclusion Unit almost as soon as he became Prime Minister – and, within months, there were a series of reports analysing the problems faced by deprived communities. New Deal for Communities (NDC) developed from these alternative strategies.

In September 1998, 32 local organisations received a letter from the Government Office North West (GONW) asking which area of Manchester they thought should be the focus of a bid for new government money, meaning the forthcoming NDC funding. The GONW wrote to housing associations, the TUC, church leaders, the CBI, the fire brigade, lots of voluntary groups and public agencies. It was a really diverse, odd group of people. We had some warning this consultation was about to happen, and although we were never told who had been contacted, we'd already written to who we thought might be on the list and lobbied them to support east Manchester. We told them we'd already been working in the area, believed in it, and thought it should be the next focus for wholesale regeneration. Everyone, without exception, wrote back and agreed with us, so we had unanimous support from the very beginning.

When we submitted our outline proposal there were only four key themes covered by the New Deal for Communities programme: poor job prospects, high levels of crime, educational under-achievement and poor health. Housing and the physical environment were left out, which was a bit bizarre. We were convinced if we tried to tackle our other problems without including housing then we'd fail. Housing and the physical environment were such big issues in east

Manchester. I think the Government felt it didn't have the resources to tackle housing, and it was some years later that Housing Market Renewal came along. But for us a stock transfer of council houses was very important and so was the ability to tackle some major issues in private sector housing. Our lobbying paid off and Whitehall did then include housing and the physical environment and it was in these areas that we subsequently had some of our first successes.

Unlike our ERCF bid, the joint bid for SRB Round 4 had been successful but had only secured a relatively small budget of £4.5 million which was shared with and administered by Tameside Metropolitan Borough Council. Together with the NDC bid we were also preparing own own bid for the fifth round of the SRB which would give us a £25 million pot just for Beswick, Clayton, and Openshaw. So by the end of 1998 we'd already submitted our outline proposals for both programmes and set up an office on Stilton Drive in the Beswick Precinct.

Of the 17 areas applying for New Deal money we were the first to apply. We'd been working towards this for some time so we were well ahead of the game. Our bid document was so well received it became a model that many of the other programmes followed, and within two months we'd been told that both outline bids – New Deal and SRB Round 5 – had been accepted.

Local residents in east Manchester had a very low opinion of the City Council at that time. They felt let down and abandoned and we had an uphill struggle convincing them that things would get better but those 12 months building relationships before the NDC programme officially started were crucial. There was a small number of groups very committed to improving their neighbourhoods and whilst they distrusted me and the Council, they were still prepared to give it a go because there was no alternative. Their area was dying on its feet and they knew it. We said we'd listen and we did listen, and we delivered what we promised to deliver. It made a huge difference.

"Don't forget, we were just ordinary people. We'd never negotiated with the town hall or anyone else before. Suddenly we were being told 'Yes, you can go to these meetings... you do have a voice... you can speak up.' It took a bit of getting used to, because you thought, 'Oh, they're not going to be mithered with us'. But the more you went, the more you realised they did listen to you. They didn't always do what you would like them to do, but they would do their best, they would try."

Doreen Burns, Beswick resident.

"I don't know how I got involved in the early days. There'd be loads of rumours flying around, so you just went to a meeting to find out what was really going on, and the next thing you know, you're involved."

Josie Fletcher, Clayton resident.

Some came on board straightaway, but with others it took a lot longer. With some, I don't think they've ever liked me or ever will. I've got no problem with that. As a servant of the Council, that's the price you pay. Sometimes you have to say 'no' and some don't like it, they take it to heart and walk away. You've got to be quite dispassionate and make decisions in the long-term interest of the whole area.

It wasn't difficult getting the level of interest initially, but channelling it was tricky. We had to ensure everyone had the opportunity to get involved and not just a small clique. So we got to work producing newsletters, organising social events and taking people on trips to other successful regeneration projects. We bought ourselves a big yellow information bus and drove it around the area, giving out leaflets and asking people about their hopes and aspirations.

There was a series of drop-in sessions and a youth information event where we played a Monopoly-type game. We gave kids £50 million and asked them to make decisions about how they'd spend their money. Things like that had never been tried before.

During 1999 local residents came up with the slogan 'Beacons for a Brighter Future' to sum up east Manchester's bid for New Deal and SRB funding. Darren Wright, ten, won a schools competition to design the logo. The local newsletter wrote, 'Our beacon is a warning that our area is in danger of decline, but also represents the good news that will come if our hard work is rewarded with the cash we need.'

So there were great celebrations in July, 1999 when the £25 million SRB funding was announced with yet more corks popping four months later when the £51.725 million New Deal money was confirmed. This time it wasn't Monopoly money and we were the first NDC in the country to secure funds. Although we unified our winnings under the Beacons banner, the combined programme has always been better known by officers and residents simply as 'New Deal'.

"I wasn't doing it for me, I was doing it for everybody, know what I mean? The first thing we realised was our little area didn't matter in the whole scheme of things, it was only a tiny cog in this massive wheel that we had to get going. We understood that, and we worked on that."

Maggie Warburton, Clayton resident.

"Everyone I met at the beginning was absolutely committed. It was mind-boggling [to me] to find a whole bunch of ordinary people from right across east Manchester who shared the same problems and who were all ready to do something about them."

Irene Johnson, Beswick resident.

During the bid process we set up six task groups to ensure residents identified specific issues and were totally involved in developing solutions. We had groups for crime and community safety; employment and training; housing and the environment; young people; health and social issues; and education. Once we were up and running these groups were crucial in monitoring our progress.

The programme was also dependent on getting the right staff in place and so I immediately started recruiting. There were colleagues I'd worked with before who I knew would be absolutely right for east Manchester and, thankfully, that's been borne out over the years.

The Government gave us about £20,000 up front to quickly set up projects and go for some 'early wins'. We did development work around neighbourhood wardens; set up a street-based cleaning team; and commissioned Groundwork's environmental work. These were relatively small-scale projects but it gave us something to get our teeth into and local people could, at last, see work had begun.

Some of the other NDCs negotiated a 'year zero', 12 months to get themselves organised, recruit staff and work out their strategy. With residents expecting immediate action we didn't get the chance for that, and within a month or so of the NDC announcement we heard we were going to get a visit from Tony Blair.

There were 30 people on our bid team. Every single agency working in east Manchester was represented as well as some of the residents' and tenants' groups. This was fine whilst it lasted, it got us to where we wanted to be, but for the Beacons board we decided it should be small and manageable. Some of the other NDCs had 35 or 40 people on their boards. There's no proper governance with that number, you just get bogged down in debate and arguments. So we decided our board would have just 12, and half of those would be residents. (More recently we've added a young person to the board so now the majority are residents.)

"Believe me, we weren't 'yes' people. No way. We were vocal... very vocal. If we didn't understand anything, we'd stop them in their tracks and ask them to explain without using jargon. 'Don't speak to us in initials; speak to us in plain English,' we'd tell them."

Linda Wagner, Beswick resident.

"The first time I got papers, I looked at them and I thought, 'Dear God in heaven, I don't understand a bloody word of this!' You know what I mean? I thought, 'Oh, I'll never do this, this is me finished.' Then I thought to myself, 'Just because you live on a council estate, you're not bloody thick! Get your head around it, concentrate on what you're doing.' And I did. Eventually with all their training and presentations we ended up knowing as much as the Council did, they'd taught us that well."

Maggie Warburton, Clayton resident.

Of the six remaining places I suggested there should be one from the voluntary sector – there have been times when this person has also been a resident – and one from the business sector. That left just four places for public agencies. We didn't want the agencies that had put so much effort into the bid to just walk away, so we set up the Public Agencies Forum. It was important, if New Deal was going to make a difference, that we challenged the way in which mainstream agencies delivered their services in east Manchester. We needed them to be involved and more accountable, and so it was the Forum who identified who should take up the remaining four places on the board.

Clearly the Council needed to be represented and Steve Mycio, the Deputy Chief Executive [formerly Director of Housing], has sat on the board from day one. That's provided useful continuity and obviously someone with his clout has been incredibly helpful. We've had someone from the housing department, from the Employment Service – later known as Jobcentre Plus – and the local police superintendent because policing was, and still is, a big issue. The housing post has since been replaced by the Primary Care Trust, but we'd periodically check with the Public Agencies Forum that the right four agencies were represented on our board.

Every spending decision has had to be agreed by the board and apart from one vote we've always come to decisions by consensus, which is remarkable. We've

"I was a resident representative on the Education Action Zone Forum which meant I became a rep on the Beacons Board. I attended task groups, steering groups and all the sub groups that came out of them. In the beginning I was attending meeting after meeting, often one immediately after another and as many as five a week. Always seeing the same faces, the same people committed to making a difference."

Irene Johnson, Beswick resident.

"They used words that we'd never heard before and, to be honest, it was a bit overwhelming at first. But they never left us out, they looked at us when they were talking to us, and if there was anything we didn't understand we were encouraged to ask... and we did."

Barbara Taylor, Beswick resident.

"They were looking for a business representative for the board and I don't think anyone else had put their hand up! Because I'd built the business up in this area, I felt it was time to give something back, and so I allowed myself to be put forward. It was a bit daunting and at first I sat and listened but have hopefully made a useful contribution since. I have a great deal of respect for the resident representatives, their impact has been fantastic over the years."

Hedley Carter, Chariot Office Supplies.

passed expensive projects like the £23 million housing stock transfer but we couldn't agree on a loan guarantee fund for the Credit Union for £5,277. I think you can get your head around what £5,277 looks like, but not £23 million!

The smooth running of the board has been largely down to the support of the staff. They've provided board members with clearly written papers, and given comprehensive presentations on the important issues so everyone has been fully informed.

In retrospect I think I would have changed the way residents were elected. Most of the other NDC areas were much smaller than east Manchester. Typically they had 4,000 properties whereas we had 20,000 residents in about 9,000 properties. So, running a straight 'one person, one vote' system would have been easier for them.

In 1999, we had about 11 or 12 residents' groups dotted around east Manchester. Mostly through the hard work of Tracey Annette [Resident Liaison Officer], this number rapidly increased. At one point there were about 65, so we've always had a strong network of groups to work with. They'd come together for the monthly Residents' Forum and it was through that Forum that representatives were elected.

There was a certain degree of accountability as most representatives felt some responsibility to the Forum and didn't get too hung up with their own self-interests. But resident associations are not the most representative of bodies. Sometimes a few very opinionated individuals dominate a small area and make it very difficult for other residents to have their say or for officers to support that area fairly.

The Government had made it clear they didn't want NDCs dominated and run by the local authorities. In east Manchester, at the time, some wards had both Labour and Liberal Democrat councillors, so including local politicians in the governance of New Deal could have been very messy. I guess there must have been some conscious decision by the City Council not to allow politics to get in the way of what we were trying to do. If councillors were also local residents they were eligible to engage in consultations and many of them sat on one or more of the task groups. I don't know how we've got away with it all these years, but I think it's been one of the reasons why it's worked so well, and one reason why residents have had a degree of trust in the process.

Sean McGonigle, NDC Co-ordinator, 1999–2009

An economy based on coal.

Production of coal in the village of Bradford – now the home of Sportcity – is first recorded at the beginning of the 17th century during the reign of James I. The coal, which is mined from shallow pits, probably supplies the entire borough of Manchester.

By the turn of the 18th century, coal mining in east Manchester drives forward the manufacturing of steel and cotton and the production of power. This is the beginning of the industrial revolution, and Manchester is its birthplace.

An East Manchester Timeline

1731

Ashton Old Road opens as a turnpike road with toll gates at Grey Mare Lane, Gorton Lane and Ogden Lane.

1740

Local landowner Sir Oswald Mosley leases 'the mine and mines, vein and veins, seam and beds of coal kannel to be found in the land around Bradford' to John Seddon of Manchester. Seddon pays Mosley £50 per year.

1773

Richard Johnson and Nephew wire works starts out as a one-man business. James Howard is a pin maker and wire drawer in Manchester who later opens a wire works. His business is bought out by John Johnson, Richard's father, who has big plans.

1841

The 1841 census shows 44 inhabitants of the village of Bradford are miners. The youngest, James Duncuff is just 10 years old. The village supplied most of the colliery's workforce until about 1870.

1846

Philips Park is created after a fundraising campaign by Mark Philips, a local MP committed to creating parks for the fast-growing urban population. The 31-acre park is one of the first municipal parks in the world.

1853

Manchester is made a city.

1854

Railway locomotive manufacturer, Beyer Peacock, starts production at the Gorton Foundry. (The first engine left the works in July 1855 built for the Great Western Railway at a cost of £2,660.)

1876

Charles Dreyfus establishes the Clayton Aniline dyeworks. (Later becomes Ciba Specialty Chemicals, and employs over 2,500 workers. The site was demolished in 2008.)

The 'Aniline' c.1900

Charles Dreyfus

Was Manchester City FC started by a woman?

Gang violence and alcoholism amongst young men in West Gorton is rife in the mid-1880s. Determined to offer an alternative, Anna Connell, the rector's daughter at St Mark's Church, and two of the churchwardens, form a cricket club in 1875. This works out well but only for as long as the season, and so the churchwardens also set up a football team – St Mark's (West Gorton) – to keep the lads busy during the winter months. In 1884, William Beastow – one of the wardens – presents the team, by now named Gorton AFC, with its first bespoke kit: black shirts with a white Maltese cross and white shorts.

In 1887 the club turns professional and renames itself Ardwick AFC as it moves to Hyde Road, its first properly enclosed ground. It isn't until 1894 that it becomes Manchester City Football Club.

1878

Newton Heath (Lancashire and Yorkshire Railway) Football Club is formed. In a strip of green and gold halves, the railway workers play on a pitch on North Road, opposite the carriage and wagon works. They enter the newly-formed football league in 1892 and move to Bank Street in Clayton a year later. (In 1902 they change their name to Manchester United, and their strip becomes red and white.)

1892

Beswick Co-operative Society formed.

A public meeting is held 'for the purpose of considering the desirability or otherwise of starting a new Co-operative Society to cater for the wants of Beswick and district – a district, large and congested, composed of working people.'

from *History of Beswick Co-operative Society Ltd., from 1892 to 1907*, by A.E. Worswick, FCIS, Secretary to the Society, 1907.

The first Beswick Co-op at 30 Ashton New Road

1904

Manchester City win the FA Cup for the first time. (Also in 1934, 1956 and 1969).

1913

The Crossley Lads' Club is established at Crossley House on Ashton Old Road by industrialist William Crossley. The building had been first used as a 'Home of Peace for Persons in Consumption'.

'On Sunday afternoons during the summers of 1918–1920 I used to visit the Short family in Stanton Street, Clayton. In those far-off days most children were barred by their parents from playing outdoor games on Sundays. We were rigged out in new clothes at Whit Week and these were worn on Sundays only until the next Whit Week. Parents would say, "Now don't forget, you can go for a nice walk this afternoon, and remember – no playing in the street." My 'nice walk' usually took me in the direction of Philips Park or Clayton. To my young mind, Clayton was rather a posh area. Beyond Bank Street one rarely saw children bare-footed, or with their breeches torn and tattered, which were common sights in the streets round where I lived.'

Frank Pritchard, *East Manchester Remembered*, 1989. Published by Neil Richardson.

In 1957, the Medical Officer of Health comments, 'The Ruhr in Germany used to have the highest fall of soot in the world. This distinction now belongs to an area covering Miles Platting, Bradford and Beswick'.

Here steam from the Stuart Street Power Station cooling towers looks like smoke in the morning sunshine. Opposite: Bradford in 1958 with the colliery winding tower, top right, and the power station, top left. (Practically every building in this photograph has since been demolished and Sportcity now occupies the site).

1966

Beyer Peacock closes in Gorton after producing nearly 8,000 railway engines in 111 years.

This is one of the last diesels in the paint shop

'Stepping out into the cold morning, I shivered a little, then made my way to Hulme Hall Lane and along Forge Lane until I arrived at the pit entrance. I handed my disc to the person in the lamp cabin, who placed it on a tally board. Next, he selected my oil lamp, lit it, then examined it carefully before handing the lamp over to me. "Careful you don't drop it or bang it, or you'll have no light," he warned me as I left. Holding the lamp in a firm grip I made my way to the pit-top and found myself in the company of miners waiting in a queue for the pit-cage. About ten miners took their positions, five on each side, stooping because of the height inside. I found myself pressed against the safety cage staring at the sides of the pit shaft and feeling a little uneasy. It is very difficult for me to describe the feelings of my first descent. The cage descended slowly for a few seconds, then it dropped at an alarming speed, my stomach turned over and my throat tightened.'

Taken from *Just Henry, Memories of Bradford and Moston Collieries, Manchester* by Henry Bairsto, 1991. Published by Neil Richardson.

1968

The winding wheel at Bradford Colliery stops forever in September 1968 as the last shift finishes. Half the 1,500 miners are redeployed in other mines. There is still plenty of coal underground but the Coal Board decide to close the mine because of substantial subsidence problems to neighbouring homes and factories.

1969

Work starts on 'Fort Beswick'.

Manchester Council had originally planned to redevelop the area in 1944 under the 'Better Beswick' plan. However, major rebuilding work does not start until 1969 when a £5 million programme is announced to build deck access flats and maisonettes for over 1,000 families. (Although inside toilets and central heating are at first welcomed by the new residents, it becomes clear within a few years that there are structural problems with the concrete blocks. The repair bill is estimated at over twice the original construction cost, so in 1982, a decision is taken to demolish the entire estate and sue the concrete supplier).

"You'd walk down the street and there'd always be five or six babies out in their prams. Their mothers would get them up, wash them and then shove them out the front. I used to come home from work for my dinner and I'd bob my head in the prams and most of the kids'd have soot all over their faces... and yet the mothers used to say it was dead healthy for the children to be getting all that fresh air! Things like that I remember."

Elaine Wright, Openshaw resident.

Deck access flats at Cablestead Walk, Beswick, 1971

1973

English Steel closes followed by Bradford Gas Works and Stuart Street Power Station in 1975, and Manchester Steel in 1985. Between 1975 and 1985 there is a 60% loss of employment, and between 1981 and 2001 there is a 22% reduction in population as residents move to find work.

1982

The East Manchester Initiative is launched.

Over the next seven years £9 million is invested in 250 schemes with the idea of demolishing derelict buildings, landscaping vacant sites and preparing land for development.

Throughout the 1980s and early 90s other initiatives follow as local politicians attempt to find a solution to spiralling decline: the East Manchester Planning Framework (1983), the East Manchester Development Strategy, the East Manchester Action Programme (1989), the East Manchester Team (1990).

18th September 1990

The International Olympic Committee vote for Atlanta as the venue for the 1996 Summer Games.

Manchester's bid for the 1996 Games is considered a toe in the water. An area of land next to the Ship Canal in Carrington is earmarked as a potential Olympic village, although no facilities are built. Manchester comes fifth out of six hopefuls, behind Atlanta, Athens, Toronto and Melbourne. Only Belgrade gets fewer votes.

1992

The East Manchester Regeneration Strategy was produced and for the first time it was identified that an international sporting event might be the catalyst needed to kick-start regeneration.

> "We had to stop having the milk delivered because it was stolen every morning; anything I planted in the garden, disappeared the next day; we went out for half an hour and the garage was broken into. It was one thing after another. If it had been just me and my husband I think we'd of stayed, but in 1993, when our son was just eight, we decided we didn't want to bring him up in Beswick. But, I didn't just move, I fled. I don't feel guilty about going, I'm proud of where I come from and there is still a strong family connection. It was such a shame it was left to get into such a state."
>
> **Cath Moran, Senior Regeneration Officer.**

23rd September 1993

At the 101st International Olympic Committee session in Monte Carlo, Sydney wins the right to host the 2000 Olympic Games after being selected over Beijing, Berlin, Istanbul and Manchester in four rounds of voting.

"We did well enough in 1990 to have another go in 1993. I remember being in the city centre the night the Olympic Committee was announcing its decision. There was a big screen in Albert Square and a real anticipation. People thought, 'We might actually do this', but the reality was we came third, which wasn't at all bad. We weren't whitewashed."

Sean McGonigle.

Spring 1994

Council Leader, Graham Stringer announces Manchester's intention to become England's nomination to host the Commonwealth Games in 2002, the Queen's Golden Jubilee Year.

September 1994

"That's our new neighbour!"

Manchester Velodrome opens – the only purpose-built indoor cycling facility in the UK.

"People didn't believe it at first. A national cycling velodrome in Clayton? No-one had even heard the word before! But building work did start on the site of the old power station and we eventually got our new neighbour. Some of us even went to the opening with Princess Anne."

Diane Vickers, Clayton resident.

The National Cycling Centre (aka Manchester Velodrome), September 1994

1994

A stretch of the A6010 (the intermediate ring road through east Manchester) is named Alan Turing Way.

Turing (1912–54) was an English mathematician, logician and cryptographer and is often considered to be the father of modern computer science. He broke the 'Enigma Code' during the Second World War and is credited for saving countless Allied lives. He was prosecuted for his homosexuality and later died from self-administered poisoning.

May 1995

Manchester's Commonwealth Games bid is submitted to the Commonwealth Games Federation.

1995

Estates Renewal Challenge Fund is created by the Conservative Government to facilitate the transfer of run-down urban council housing to new landlords which could include local housing associations.

November 1995

The Commonwealth Games Federation award Manchester the XVIIth Commonwealth Games. Manchester City Council decide to prioritise east Manchester in relation to any future regeneration activity and funding.

"Nobody really believed it, they said, 'Oh, give over! You've got to be joking!' But I have to take my hat off to the City Council. They worked miracles. They did a good job."

Doreen Burns, Beswick resident.

Jubilation in Albert Square as the Games decision is announced

15th June 1996

IRA bomb explodes in Manchester city centre.

Nothing for the kids.

"In 1996, when I first started working in east Manchester, there were two problems that consistently troubled residents. One was kids and the other was crime.

"Parents were worried about everything to do with their children, at every age. There were no parent and toddler groups, the schools were failing them, there was no youth provision, nothing. So the children were bored and under-achieving... and getting up to no good.

"The issues around crime were largely to do with nuisance crime. Neighbour nuisance was a big issue: everything from gardens being left in a complete mess to burnt-out cars left on footpaths."

Claire Evans, 4CT Chief Executive (former JOG Co-ordinator).

May 1997

Labour come to power and in December Prime Minister Tony Blair creates the Social Exclusion Unit to examine 'how to develop an integrated and sustainable approach to the problems of the worst housing estates, including crime, drugs, unemployment, community breakdown and bad housing.'

19th September 1997

Meeting held at St Jerome's Church in Beswick to talk about a bid for Single Regeneration Budget Round 4 and Estates Renewal Challenge Fund. Very angry and vociferous residents at the meeting include Wendy Eaton, Rita Birch and Elaine Wright from Higher Openshaw Residents' Association; Sheila Rhodes, Stan Pargeter and Veronica Powell from Beswick resident groups; and Reverend Roy Chow.

In the Beginning.

"There were lots of feral youths about, property was getting damaged, cars were being stolen, and gangs were hanging around. It just felt uncomfortable. It wasn't serious crime, that's crept up on us since, it was nuisance, petty crime."

Barbara Taylor, Beswick resident.

"We had a lot of problems with social landlords. They'd take anybody in for a rent cheque and they didn't give a damn about the area. It backfired on some of them because their tenants wrecked the properties so badly that they just got boarded up."

Steve Green, Openshaw resident.

The houses round here were an absolute bloody shambles. So in my infinite wisdom, I decided to have a go at the housing association... and the Council...and the police, and anybody else that I thought needed kicking up the arse. We didn't deserve this. All we were asking for was a decent street to live in and for them to do the job that they were getting paid for."

Maggie Warburton, Clayton resident.

"I think the turning point, as I say, was realising that we weren't on our own. I used to think it was only us that was having trouble with them breaking into our car, trying to break into our house. And yet, everyone had it, but no-one was sharing that information at first."

Wendy Eaton, Openshaw resident.

"It was really quite desolate at that time. We were in a consultation meeting in Beswick one evening and outside there was a young child – and he was only a child – driving a stolen car round and round in circles, trying to burn out the engine."

Rachel Downey, regeneration consultant to Manchester City Council.

"None of the agencies that were supposed to be working in the area were actually doing anything. If the police did bother to come out, nothing ever got done. At that time my public enemy number one was the housing association. They'd move disaffected families into their homes but there was never any attempt to manage them."

Elaine Wright, Openshaw resident.

"We noticed that the area was looking neglected but put that down to the Thatcher legacy and massive unemployment. We had no need to wander around the estate as we used to when the children were young, we tended to just get in the car and go to work. So it came as a shock when we realised things were much worse than we'd thought. The place was falling apart and we hadn't noticed. My daughter – who lived close by with her own family – told me that as the older neighbours died, they were replaced by young people who were abusing drugs. These were people we had seen looking harassed and depressed and had assumed unemployment and poverty was the cause. I suppose the drug-taking has a lot to do with poverty and depression but many of our original neighbours had lived through the financial crisis of the 1930s without resorting to drugs."

Irene Johnson, Beswick resident.

"When my children were growing up I used to worry about the lad getting involved in gangs. He's always been car mad, so I used to hope to God he'd never get in with the local car thieves. When he was about 14, my husband, Alf, bought him an old banger which we had here on the front, and he'd spend hours tinkering with it. That was great because we knew where he was and we could keep an eye on him. He's a mechanic in a local garage now."

June Webb, Beswick resident.

19th February

Disappointed but not surprised.

A letter is sent from Hilary Armstrong, Minister for Local Government and Housing, to local MP Tony Lloyd explaining why the ERCF bid had been turned down. (See page 10.)

(See page 10.)

19 98

April

Hilary Armstrong visits east Manchester and attends residents' meetings to explain the decision to turn down ERCF but talks about a new regeneration initiative being developed.

"We were a bit deflated when she said we weren't getting the Estates Fund. She said, 'We're bringing in something called New Deal for Communities. It's a package of measures, it's not just about throwing money at bricks and mortar.' As it turned out, it was the best thing for us.

"I always remember Hilary Armstrong turning round and saying, 'Don't be afraid to try new things. If you fail, at least you've tried.' And we did try new things: some didn't work at all well and some worked brilliantly and have now gone citywide."

Barbara Taylor, Beswick resident.

August

East Manchester Residents' Forum set up. Resident Liaison Officer Tracey Annette pulls together the dozen or so existing residents' groups to form an 'umbrella' forum that meets monthly and elects resident representatives to the various boards. More groups are encouraged to set up and eventually the forum has a membership of over 50.

"Looking back, I would have liked us to have been more open. As well as the residents' groups, imagine what we could have done if we'd got church groups involved, and play groups, and parent-teacher associations. Perhaps we couldn't have managed all that. We did have the Task Groups and events like Parties in the Park and other consultation events that maybe filled that gap."

Tracey Annette, former Resident Liaison Officer.

"I set up the business back in 1977 just as east Manchester was declining as an economic powerhouse. Early on Johnson and Nephew wire works was one of our best customers and we really felt the effect of its closure. I bought this shop in 1984 when there was still plenty of heavy engineering on the site opposite but when the 2000 Olympic Games bid was announced the whole site had to be cleared and leveled – everything was compulsory purchased – so it looked as if progress was being made. When that bid failed, it left this great, empty expanse and made the whole area feel more depressed than it already was."

Hedley Carter, Chariot Office Supplies.

The Sportcity site cleared and awaiting development, August 1998

11th–21st September

Kuala Lumpur hosts the XVI Commonwealth Games with first-class facilities and excellent organisation. Manchester City Council officials attend and take note.

18th September

Letter from Government Office North West to 32 organisations in Manchester announcing the launch of NDC, and asking them to form a partnership and decide which area of Manchester should be the focus of the programme.

December

First phase outline NDC proposal submitted.

10th December

Richard Caborn, Minister for the Environment, visits east Manchester and meets residents at Mill Street Venture Centre.

"He tells us that we can take risks and that failure is an option. He's since confided to me that he found some of the strong women he met terrifying. They clearly left an impression on him!"

Sean McGonigle.

"He was one of the first to come up and I was delighted to tell him what we wanted. We wanted decent streets and decent houses. We didn't want any bloody statues, no fancy ornaments all over the estate for dogs to widdle up!"

Maggie Warburton, Clayton resident.

15th December

NDC office opens at 17 Stilton Drive and includes drinks and food for residents. Resident Stan Pargeter attends dressed as Father Christmas, drinks too much and falls asleep.

18th December

Outline SRB bid is successful and a detailed bid is invited.

January

Letter from Richard Caborn, Minister for the Environment and Hilary Armstrong, Minister for Local Government and Housing, to say the first phase NDC bid has been successful.

1999

"We knew we'd done our best with the bids. There was a long-term plan and a clear vision, and you felt, with the Games on the horizon, something quite meaningful was about to happen."

Rachel Downey, regeneration consultant to Manchester City Council.

January

Openshaw Youth Conference at Crossley House, followed later in the month by Beswick Youth Conference at Ardwick Lads Club and the Clayton Youth Conference at Clayton Youth Club.

Local youngsters enjoy discos, free food, face painting, raffles, football contests, hair and nail art, and get the chance to spend £50 million in 'East Manchester Monopoly'.

26th February

The bids are going well so a celebration event is held at Manchester Velodrome for residents, staff and partners. For most, this is the first time they've set foot in the National Cycling Centre. It's a cold night so there's hotpot on the menu.

"The local perception of the velodrome was quite negative from the start. Here was this elite cycling venue, hosting international meetings with cyclists coming from all over the world, right in the middle of run-down Clayton. Local people were disrupted during its construction and many saw it as a white elephant. There was a 'not for us' attitude which we had to resolve and make sure wasn't repeated when the stadium was built.

"When NDC got started we'd hold residents meetings there, and job fairs and community sports events, anything to get people through the doors so they could see for themselves what a wonderful facility it could be for them. On one occasion there was schools' basketball in the centre of the track, a netball competition outside in the car park, a health walking club doing circuits of the concourse and then, on the track itself, the GB cycling team training. Now that's a community facility."

Sean McGonigle.

3rd March
Tessa Jowell MP visits east Manchester and meets partners at the NDC office to talk about Sure Start.

30th April
Single Regeneration Budget Round 5 bid is submitted.

11th May
A series of consultation drop-in events start with one at St Cross Church in Clayton.

It's good to talk: consultation in Clayton   Hilary Armstrong visits Beswick

12th May
Hilary Armstrong MP visits again and meets residents, board members and partners at the School of the Resurrection in Beswick. She has a private meeting with residents.

"When we came into government in 1997 there was a clear understanding that we had to look at ways to effectively tackle the issues of disadvantaged communities. The Social Exclusion Unit – which Tony Blair established and which came under my remit – did that in a number of ways.

"We had 18 Policy Action Teams looking at specific areas like education and financial inclusion and for each we brought together top-class thinkers, practitioners and residents who worked with the Civil Service to develop a strategy. Government had not worked like this before, certainly not in recent history, and people were very excited by this approach. It was out of those teams that NDC was born.

"Given my history as a community worker I was convinced the model we inherited from the Tories was weighed too far towards physical regeneration with not enough emphasis on people. You can tart up the environment as much as you like, and yes, that's important, but you also have to involve local people. They have to live the change. Unless you enable them to develop skills and to take more control over their communities then the regeneration is likely not to work.

"I was absolutely committed to making sure the people who lived in these area had a say in how they were going to be regenerated and that we established other developments to make sure residents grew with their communities. Everyone has the capacity to develop. What NDC could do was offer them a situation where they could develop more effectively. That's what the government's job is: to create the conditions in which people can make the best of themselves and that's what we were about.

"In Manchester I remember residents' anger at the way things had been left to deteriorate, but also a determination to stay and to see things improve. It was also clear to me that local agencies weren't used to working together and we understood we weren't going to change an area without engaging all the stakeholders.

"Yes, we did encourage new ways of working and yes, it was acceptable to fail from time to time. You can't succeed at everything but if you don't try you'll always be left wondering. But there needs to be a balance: if everything you try fails then you lose heart... so you need strong leadership to maintain a good balance."

Hilary Armstrong MP, Minister of State with responsibility for Local Government and Housing, 1997–2001.

15th July

The SRB announcement is made and east Manchester gets £25 million! There's an impromptu celebration with Council Leader Richard Leese, Director of Housing Steve Mycio and local residents in a back alley near Ravensbury School.

14th August

Community consultation day in the semi-derelict Grange to gather opinions on potential future uses.

"There was me, Doreen Burns and Sheila Rhodes at a task group meeting and we were saying, 'We've got all this money and we haven't even got a community centre.' We said to Sean, 'What's happening with the Grange, can we go and have a look?' That was how it all started. We had to have a feasibility study done and so we had an open day and invited everyone to come and have a say on what they wanted. Oh I remember! It was hanging! It was damp, it stank, there were mushrooms growing everywhere, there was no hot water. I was carrying buckets of hot water from here to there, scrubbing, trying to get it cleaned up."

Barbara Taylor, Beswick resident.

17th September

NDC bid is submitted, one of only two to meet the early deadline.

29th October

Birth of New East Manchester Ltd.

Hilary Armstrong MP does the honours at MANCAT (later The Manchester College) and is then taken on a tour.

"The Urban Regeneration Company (URC) model flowed from an appreciation – an undertaking, if you like – for a delivery vehicle to take strategic ownership of east Manchester over the longer term. That appreciation was developed from our experience both in Hulme and in the city centre after the bomb. The URC has a very specific focus to restructure the economic base, revitalise the housing market and get local people into work, not just in the New Deal neighbourhoods but in the wider east Manchester area."

Eddie Smith, Chief Executive, New East Manchester.

10th November

Here's another £51.725 million!

Announcement of successful NDC bid so another impromptu celebration, this time on Beswick Precinct. East Manchester is the first NDC to secure funding.

Announcements are made at the same time that east Manchester is to become an Education Action Zone and Clayton would have a Sure Start programme.

"We were listening for the announcement on the radio and when it came through it all went a bit manic. Elaine got on the phone and told everyone the news and we started making a banner with felt tips and pictures printed from the computer. I remember Sean – who'd been at the radio station – walking in and finding us on our knees colouring this giant roll of paper. It was all very exciting and, by the time we'd finished and the photographer had arrived, there was quite a crowd for that picture."

Tracey Annette, former Resident Liaison Officer.

"One of the reasons I came to east Manchester was because I felt we'd learnt a lot in Hulme and Moss Side about how we could do things better. I thought if we could do things slightly differently we might achieve even more. For instance, in Hulme and Moss Side we'd done well at engaging the local community but only around housing issues. For me there was potential to engage the local community in a whole lot more. What would happen if we involved communities in education, in health, or in the provision of local services? We could do all that in east Manchester.

"I'd worked in this city for 20 years before I set foot in east Manchester. Why would you come? I had to use the A-Z to find Beswick on that first bleak, rainy morning. As I pulled up next to the precinct, a skip was on fire and three kids were throwing bricks at an Alsatian. It was unbelievable.

"But it wasn't just how it looked... there wasn't a single spark of energy about the place. People who were paid to work in east Manchester were almost defeated by their everyday struggle to make a difference. Many were fed up and worn down, they were on their knees.

"I thought, oh yes, we can do something here. We just need a dream team, and that's what we got."

Libby Graham, Director of Social Programmes. (She had previously worked with Sean McGonigle on Hulme City Challenge and in the Moss Side and Hulme Partnership).

12th November

Time for a knees-up!

Residents, staff and residents gather at the Donaheys club in Clayton to toast their double funding win: £25 million from SRB and £51.725 from NDC.

"Many of the staff, including myself, had come from the town hall where the relationship between officers and residents was very detached. That party at Donaheys was an eye-opener for me – getting to know residents socially – and it set the tone for a totally different relationship. From then on we were a team and that single event seemed to mark the start of a new culture of working together."

Lesley Spencer, Principal Regeneration Officer.

Sean McGonigle and resident Josie Fletcher hit the dance floor

December

Police use new legislation for the first time in Manchester to tackle endemic antisocial behaviour.

"There were three boys who caused mayhem in one particular neighbourhood. The family was involved in heavy duty intimidation with a gang around them. They would steal people's things and then sell them back to them. Tenants left in droves. The family were evicted from the area but continued to return. After two years and evidence from local agency staff and some very brave tenants, the police secured one of the first antisocial behaviour orders. When they appealed the community were terrified, but I am glad to say they lost three appeals."

Sean McGonigle.

"We'd heard stories saying who was causing the problems but no statements saying what they had done. We had to work hard to get behind the wall of silence, particularly on this problem family. They exerted enormous peer pressure on other kids to get into crime.

"Once the ASBO was passed, local facilities started to be used more. People started to go back to the places that had been terrorised – the library, the shopping precinct. This family had affected the whole local economy."

Superintendent Dave Thompson.

6th December

Prime Minister Tony Blair and Mo Mowlam MP visit east Manchester. After laying a foundation stone at the stadium site they meet the six Resident Board Representatives at Barbara Taylor's home, before walking through Beswick to the NDC offices on Stilton Drive above the precinct.

"I wasn't allowed to tell anyone who was coming, I just had to say it was a ministerial visit and that we'd be told nearer the time who it was. We planned for him to come to Barbara Taylor's house in Beswick and I think everyone guessed it was the Prime Minister because the police had the sniffer dogs out and were checking everything. "Before he came to us he'd been to lay a foundation stone on the stadium site which – as construction hadn't yet begun – was still a big muddy field. It was about half four on a cold, wet, miserable December afternoon when his cavalcade arrived at Barbara's house and she and I went out with umbrellas to meet him and Mo Mowlam. We all crammed into Barbara's kitchen with five other resident representatives and all the paparazzi and reporters. He had a cup of tea and we all had a good chat although it was a bit false with all the press there.

"When he came out he said, 'Where next?' and when I said we were going back to our office he said, 'Okay, let's go!' and set off walking instead of getting back in the cars which had been the plan. By this time the word had got out and there were lots of residents, mainly kids, chasing after us, getting him to sign autographs. The Special Branch was having kittens, charging along in front of us trying to clear the way. He was like the Pied Piper of Hamelin!

"At that time Beswick was a bit rough to say the least. We passed some recently burnt-out houses and a well-known drugs den. It was all a bit surreal escorting the Prime Minister amongst all that deprivation with half of east Manchester following behind!

"Before he left he announced he'd be back in 18 months to see the progress we'd made. That raised expectations even further."

Sean McGonigle.

January

Work starts on the construction of the City of Manchester Stadium.

21st January

Tenant Participation Advisory Service conference in Manchester. Clayton resident Maggie Warburton speaks in public for the first time and is marked ten out of ten by delegates.

"Once I'm off talking about east Manchester, I'm away in a transit. It's from my heart. They said it went down all right but you can never tell when you're standing up there like a bloody idiot. But, I enjoyed it."

January

East Manchester Education Action Zone is established.

The Education Action Zone is the major programme charged with raising education standards in all east Manchester schools. The Zone will recruit, train and support staff in schools to raise attainment, improve attendance and widen opportunities for all pupils. It has a £4.1 million budget over its five-year lifetime.

There's a huge musical and sports knees-up at the velodrome on 6th March to mark the launch of the Zone attended by 17 schools and 500 pupils.

24th January

Minister for Sport, Kate Hoey MP, makes a brief visit to the velodrome to look at preparations for the Commonwealth Games.

25–26th January

A small group of east Manchester residents and officers attend the first NDC conference in Brighton.

Hilary Armstrong MP tells delegates: "You are pathfinders, pioneers not only for New Deal for Communities but for neighbourhood renewal nationally.

"I am confident that, with the continuing hard work of all those involved, you will change these neighbourhoods dramatically over the next ten years."

East Manchester and Shoreditch in London have already secured funding and a further £370 million grants for eight more deprived communities are announced at the conference:

· Birmingham (Kings Norton) £3 million (for a further year of development work)
· Bradford (Little Horton) £50 million
· Bristol (Barton Hill) £50 million
· Leicester (Braunstone) £49.5 million
· London (Southwark) £56.2 million
· London (Newham, West Ham and Plaistow) £54.6 million
· Sandwell (Greets Green) £56 million
· West Middlesbrough £52.1 million

"One of the reasons we had the conferences was to allow people to share their experiences. If you've lived in a failing area for many years, you are probably not going to have the necessary skills to motivate others or the knowledge of projects elsewhere to know what might work in your area. That was one of my passions: if you encouraged residents to meet with others going through the same experiences, it would give them the added confidence to make changes."

Hilary Armstrong MP, Minister of State with responsibility for Local Government and Housing, 1997–2001.

Born in the shadow of English Steel in Openshaw, with factory trains wending their way through terraced streets, Dot Rathbone has always been an activist. She's championed the rights of ordinary people and represented them on the local council. When she retired to sheltered accommodation in Ancoats, her work continued.

I was a child of a mixed marriage. My mother had God and my father had the union! So politics was always with us. My dad and I would talk for hours and hours... about everything.

I joined the Labour Party when I was 18. My first campaign was opposing the merger of our local school with a failing one. We set up a parent–teachers group to fight that decision and it was eventually overturned. I was then asked to help in the local advice centre here in Ancoats, supposedly just for a couple of weeks. I was there for 27 years! We'd help people fill in forms, fight for their rights, and get what they were entitled to.

After I divorced I bought a house in Levenshulme that was falling down. What a nightmare that was! Me and the kids were living there while it was being renovated around us. Both my children were very academic and I got grants to send them to independent schools. I was dreading telling my dad but he was fine about it: "It's their future that's important," he said.

After they'd both gone off to university I was rattling around the house like a pea in a drum, so decided to get more involved with the Labour Party. The local elections came up and I was encouraged to stand. I thought I had no chance. But I won! I served on Manchester City Council for eight years until 1999.

I always fancied moving here when I retired, so I put my name on the waiting list. After a while a flat became vacant and I moved in... and I love it! But I didn't stop campaigning. The place was so grotty at first and yet there was so much potential, especially with the garden.

First we worked with New Deal to set up a residents' committee so we could apply for funds. The path down the side was dark and dangerous, so we applied for an environmental improvement grant and had it resurfaced and new lighting installed. That was our first success and that benefited the whole community, not just Mayes Gardens.

Then we got grants to improve the community room and the communal laundry, then new chairs for the exercise room, a zebra crossing on the main road and so on. Oh, and then there's our Days Out for Recycled Teenagers, but that's another story. (See page 150).

February

The beginnings of Eastserve...

"I was invited to meet with a communications consultant who was proposing the development of a 'virtual town hall', where residents could access services and information via the fledgling world wide web. In our delivery plan for New Deal we'd already identified information technology as a major tool for resident involvement... we just weren't sure how we were going to do it at that time."

Sean McGonigle.

March

East Manchester Credit Union established.

79% of residents are on at least one benefit, doorstep lending is rife, and there are no banks or ATMs in east Manchester.

"We were originally the Beswick and Openshaw Credit Union, serving maybe only 100 members who all knew each other. In 2000, our chair, Tim Presswood, recognised that credit unions needed to be more professional if they were to attract new members. He won funding which paid for my position and allowed us to open a shop on Beswick Precinct where we had a higher profile. That's when we changed our name to the East Manchester Credit Union."

Christine Moore, Manchester Credit Union.

7th March

Starter for ten.

First quiz night held at the Townley Pub, Beswick as a team-building event between residents, staff and agencies. The gloves are off: everyone is out to win.

10th March

Staff team-building event held at the Orangery at Heaton Park: residents were the most important people.

"It wasn't typically council. We were very adaptable. It was about doing things differently, bringing about change... and listening to people. We never said it wasn't our problem, if we couldn't help then we'd find someone who could. That was our ethos, and I liked that way of working. I got the bug."

Cath Moran, Senior Regeneration Officer.

"There was a feeling amongst the east Manchester team that we were the best at everything we did, and you believed you were. We had a really good team, and people who didn't fit in – maybe they had the wrong attitude towards the community – didn't seem to stay. If their style wasn't our style, they moved on."

Tracey Annette, former Resident Liaison Officer.

"If you didn't show empathy and understanding of what people lived through in east Manchester you could expect a tongue-lashing from any one of the resident representatives... and rightly so."

Paul Cullen, former Community Safety Co-ordinator.

22nd March

Deputy Prime Minister John Prescott MP visits Manchester and announces £289 million government funding to extend Metrolink. A new route to Ashton would see trams running to Sportcity in time for the Commonwealth Games.

30th March

Public Agencies Forum meets for the first time. Four agencies are represented on the Beacons Board (see page 15), and others are kept on track through the Forum.

"They were all interested because we had money to spend and everyone wanted a piece of the pie. We used the funding as a 'carrot' to encourage them to do some great work."

Lesley Spencer, Principal Regeneration Officer.

12th April

Beverley Hughes MP, Junior Minister in the Home Office, visits to launch the Cross Tenure Neighbour Nuisance Team, the first in the country.

"We'd see them getting evicted from one place and literally going round the corner and moving into a private landlord. And they carry on still, the trouble's still there, it never moves away."

Maggie Warburton, Clayton resident.

"Honestly, that was one of the most significant things NDC ever did. When that team was set up, people realised that, ultimately, they could be evicted if they didn't change their ways. They might not have been bothered about being in trouble with the police, but there were bothered about losing their home. That brought a lot of people into line."

Barbara Taylor, Beswick resident.

"Residents said they wanted a locally-based team that would intervene as soon as problems arose and continue to be involved over the long-term... and that's just what they got."

Jackie Hynes, Community Safety Manager, Eastlands Homes.

"It wasn't just about your next door neighbour playing loud music, it was about a whole range of problems that affect a community. This team has taught us a lot about dealing with nuisance across tenure."

Paul Cullen, former Community Safety Co-ordinator.

13th April

Off to visit the Bromley by Bow Centre in London to learn from pioneering projects including their Healthy Living Centre.

2nd and 3rd May

Fact-finding in Holland.

Residents and officers visit Amsterdam to investigate a range of projects: neighbourhood wardens, home zones, and an intensive support employment project.

"It was clear we didn't have all the answers when we first started, but we knew there were places we could visit which were examples of best practice. So we visited the Pennywell Estate in Sunderland, the Eldonians in Liverpool, the Bromley by Bow Centre in London, Royds Estate in Bradford and then, in May 2000, we went to Amsterdam."

"There were about 12 residents and about eight staff who went for two days. It wasn't expensive – we flew with a budget airline and stayed in a basic hotel – but, of course, we were criticised for that trip. For me, its purpose was clear. We learnt some important lessons from the Dutch projects and, by spending time with our residents, it helped to build trust between us."

Sean McGonigle.

June

"We were offered a coach for the day for a resident group outing. Instead of a theme park I decided we'd go to Sale Water Park where they were having a 'countryside day' with pond dipping, craft events and a parade! Most of the kids on our estate would probably not have experienced anything like that before so off we all went, all age groups, with our butties and drinks. Oh! the horror on people's faces when we descended on the park."

Irene Johnson, Beswick resident.

3rd June

National Volunteers' Week celebrations at the 'Pitz'.

"It was an awards evening in recognition of all our hardworking volunteers. We bought some replica Oscars from Afflecks Palace in town – they looked the business but weren't as heavy, obviously. We wanted to make it a bit of a laugh and so Sheila Rhodes said she would ask if her cousin, Frank (better known as the drag queen Foo Foo Lamarr), would present the gongs. We were thrilled when she said he'd do it!

"On the night it got later and later and 'Our Frank', as Sheila called him, hadn't turned up. She got on the phone and it turned out his big gold Rolls Royce – his trademark – had broken down and so I offered to fetch him from town. Sean came with me in my little Metro and we parked on double yellow lines as I dashed into his club in the Gay Village. There he was in front of me: fully made up and at least seven feet tall in his heels and bouffant wig. He was totally in character from the minute I met him.

"When he saw the car he said, cheekily, 'How the hell am I going to get into that heap of ****!' With Sean in the back, 'Our Frank' did manage to get in, although his hair was too tall and he had to sit with his head at an angle and his beehive sticking in my face the whole time. It was a scream! Then one of his false nails came off... and every time I looked in the mirror there was Sean creased up in the back. It was a great night!"

Lesley Spencer, Principal Regeneration Officer.

8th June

Junior Minister Angela Eagle MP opens the Step Ahead Employment and Training Support Centre at Beswick Precinct.

16th June

Another visit by Junior Minister Beverley Hughes MP, this time to meet residents and discuss crime and antisocial behaviour.

"In 1998 a police officer turned up to a resident's house in Openshaw after she'd been burgled and said, 'What do you expect living here? I'd just move if I were you.' That was typical of the relationship at that time between the police and the people they were meant to serve. Residents were having a horrendous experience but no-one was listening to them.

"The NDC money meant we could pay to get the police on our side. Nowadays we have neighbourhood police teams but ten years ago it was very different. Then there was a mutual distrust: the police and the Council had only just started talking to each other. We didn't work together, or have common targets as we do now. NDC changed all that.

"Working so closely with the residents was an eye-opener. To have them coming straight into the office, up to your desk and talking directly to you was unheard of in the Council. It was strange for about a month and then, after that, I couldn't imagine working without the residents. It was extremely useful. They had an insight we could never have: ideas about what they needed, what they wanted us to deliver, where we were falling down.

"I remember one police office said to me early on, 'Having residents round the table keeps you honest.' And it was true. It was invaluable."

Paul Cullen, former Community Safety Co-ordinator.

3rd July

The Showcase Cinema on Hyde Road is hired to show *East is East* which was shot in the Toxteth Street area of Higher Openshaw. Local residents cook Asian food back at the Church of the Resurrection in Beswick and discuss the issues around race and equality raised by the film.

6th July

Paymaster General Dawn Primarolo MP pays a visit.

"Oh, everybody came: the dog and the horse with 'em."

September

East Manchester secures Sport Action Zone status.

Funded by Sport England through the National Lottery, the SAZ is 'designed to address the lack of sports activities and facilities in some of the most socially and economically deprived areas of the country and to bring the benefits of sport and physical activity to these communities.' East Manchester's SAZ will run for five years.

"Before 2000 there was a dearth of sporting facilities in east Manchester. Parks were run down and none had playgrounds or sports pitches. The only thriving sporting clubs were crown green bowling, boxing clubs and a couple of football clubs.

"We wanted to encourage a greater diversity of sports, especially those popular with young people, and to train and support local people – usually parents – to start new clubs. Nowadays there are dozens of new clubs, from cheerleaders to junior football, and literally thousands of children and young people doing sport each week, which is a wonderful legacy.

"Every primary school in the area now has excellent play facilities, many available to community groups after hours, and the parks all have new playgrounds and kickabout areas... it's been an amazing turnaround."

John Dwan, former Sport Action Zone Manager.

Before New Deal there were few opportunities for east Manchester's young people

New Deal's ten-year programme has coincided with rapid advances in the digital revolution. Computer ownership and internet access have not only become mainstream but now an integral part of daily life. For the New Deal team, then, keeping residents ahead in this fast-moving 'cyber world' has been yet another challenge. Sean McGonigle tells the Eastserve story:

In 1999, not only were the majority of residents in Beswick, Clayton and Openshaw socially excluded, but – with the digital revolution taking hold – they were at risk of being digitally excluded too. We recognised this threat early and included an aspiration in our initial plans for access to computers and widespread training, although we had no idea, at the time, how we would achieve either.

Our first presence on the web was an interactive 'portal' where residents could request housing repairs, fill in a CV template, or even anonymously report crime. These initiatives were only useful if people could access the web and our first survey was worrying, if not a surprise. Only 19% of residents had use of a computer either at home or at work, against a national average of over 50%.

The Government launched initiatives to tackle digital exclusion and we took full advantage of everything on offer. The Computers Within Reach programme allowed us to work with the social enterprise ITEM (Information Technology in East Manchester) to distribute 350 reconditioned computers. Later, with the Wired Up Communities project, we were able to expand that offer by a factor of ten.

But we weren't just about to give away computers. We offered subsidised PCs for £200 (the retail price was nearer £1,000 in 2001); we insisted everyone who bought a computer undertook some basic training first; and we introduced thousands to the web with three months' free dial-up access.

It was a huge success. 3,500 residents took up our offer although few had the money. The majority also took out an instant, low interest loan from the local credit union which was underwritten by New Deal. Our IT programme was now well established under the name Eastserve, with premises on the Beswick Precinct.

Training thousands of residents would have been more of a challenge had it not been for the UK Online programme which funded training 'hubs' in informal settings like community centres and schools, as well as the local college.

Yes, the training programme was about IT skills but it had the added benefit of getting people back into the learning mindset – for many their school experiences had been far from positive – giving them the confidence to take things further. MANCAT (later The Manchester College) reported that 800 Eastserve customers had progressed to other courses and qualifications.

New Deal has always been about involving local people and Eastserve was no exception. Volunteering has been a central part of the project: some residents contributed content to the now rebranded eastserve.com website; others moderated chat rooms; whilst the more technically minded were trained to offer support either by phone or in person.

By now computer ownership and training were on track, but with the popularity of mobile phones, new technical complications emerged. Fewer and fewer residents had a landline so could not access a dial-up service. A new solution was needed which came in the form of a localised wireless network. Well before broadband services became widely available, Eastserve customers could choose between a range of packages, with no contract or connection fee.

But the digital world never stands still and Eastserve has had to adapt in a competitive marketplace. Crucially the service has remained local, true to its roots and has, on the whole, enjoyed a good reputation. It is the only service in east Manchester available to a substantial proportion of residents who no longer have a landline telephone.

5,500 residents have purchased a subsidised computer and over 6,000 have received basic computer training.

4,000 have been connected to the wireless broadband network and 1,600 remain regular paying customers.

Computer ownership has grown from 19% in 2001 to 57% in 2008.

"We've still got our Eastserve computer. It's knackered now and we're due a new one but we've had that for eight years! Eastserve has been a good service: very accessible and affordable, which is what it's about really."

Andrea Melarkey, Clayton resident.

"Eastserve, in my opinion, was the best thing to come out of New Deal for Communities. I was over 60, retired, and had never even turned a computer on and now I couldn't live without it. I did all the publicity material for the Beacons Women's Network on my computer... and I've been an Eastserve subscriber from the beginning. People who would never have had a chance of owning a computer were able to buy one through the credit union... it was a great opportunity."

Sandra Black, Beswick resident.

In 2001 Eastserve offered subsidised computers with internet connection to east Manchester residents for a fraction of their retail value. Shirley Hughes was one of hundreds who took up the offer, unaware that it was to change her life.

I've always been interested in how things work. As a girl I'd play with Meccano and later tinker with motorbikes or build something for the house. When the Eastserve offer came through the door, I jumped at the chance. I thought it would help the children with their schoolwork and I liked the idea of playing around with a computer, finding out how it worked.

When it arrived I was on it day and night! I researched how computers worked on the internet and found out everything there was to know about operating them. When I wasn't in front of the screen, I was reading computer books. I was hooked!

After about six months I was invited by Eastserve to become one of their volunteer helpers — community champions, they called them — who would assist other residents with their technical queries. We'd have a rota system with calls routed to our own homes where we'd offer telephone support. If we couldn't help them over the phone, we'd arrange a visit.

Of course MANCAT ran courses for the Eastserve customers and I lapped them up. On one occasion, one of the trainers asked if I'd stand in and do a training session, which I did. They then asked if I'd consider doing a teacher training qualification and so I did a short course and the next thing I knew I was being offered a job at the college as a full-time trainer!

The first course I taught was Women into Technology, for residents who had completed some basic computer training but wanted to know more. We'd look at Microsoft Office, learn about Word and Excel, how to use the internet, send emails, that sort of thing. We also did a short repair and maintenance course, so my first students all got an extra qualification as well.

I'm still teaching at the same college – it's now called The Manchester College – and I'm the IT Trainer here for the Business Training Department. We've trained many other residents who have started off with Eastserve, people like me who have wanted to know more, and have gone on to better things.

The computer bug has certainly bitten me: I *love* playing with computers. So this is the perfect job for me. I get to play with computers every day!

12th September

Home Secretary Charles Clarke MP comes to east Manchester to hear from the local police and to listen to residents.

16th September–1st October

Sydney 2000 Summer Olympic Games.

"Up until the early 1990s the Commonwealth Games weren't regarded as that great a sporting spectacle. Even the Games in Victoria, Canada in 1994 were very low-key, very provincial, and nothing to compare with the Olympics. But then, as Manchester was preparing for its turn, Kuala Lumpur hosted a fantastic Games in 1998 with an Olympic-style atmosphere, great crowds, TV audiences and many more sports. Two years later Sydney staged an amazing Olympics and so by the time it was Manchester's turn it felt as if the bar had been raised and there were great expectations on us."

Sean McGonigle.

October

The eastern junctions 19–24 of the M60 open, completing Manchester's orbital motorway.

November

Consultation event at the Toxteth Street Baptist Church, Higher Openshaw with Sean McGonigle and Libby Graham from New Deal for Communities, and Family Housing Association (later Adactus).

17th December

NDC team move to their new offices at Grey Mare Lane.

"At first we said it would end up like a mini town hall, but we got assurances that it was for the local people and that's proved to be true."

Doreen Burns, Beswick resident.

"For a lot of people that office was a one-stop shop. They felt they could walk in off the street and ask almost anything, and they could. There was no reception counter, residents could go up to someone's desk and we'd help."

Tracey Annette, former Resident Liaison Officer.

"Once you walk through their front door it's like being slowly kidnapped... but in a nice way. You might have just gone in to ask a question but once they realise you're interested in what's going on and have got something to offer the rest of the community, they won't let you go. I walked into their offices in 2000, by 2002 I'd become a member of the board and two years later I was chair, and have been ever since."

Irene Baron, Clayton resident.

"We'd walk round with residents and position street lights in areas they wanted them, not where we thought they needed them. There was a lot of collaboration."

Paul Cullen, former Community Safety Co-ordinator.

January

National Strategy Action Plan published.

Between 1999 and 2000, the Government set up 18 Policy Action Teams to look at specific areas of deprivation (education, financial inclusion, neighbourhood management etc). The teams are made up of government officials, academics, residents and local professionals: experts in their fields to assess what is needed in disadvantaged communities. Their conclusions feed into the National Strategy Action Plan and the NDC programme is part of this strategy.

28th March

Launch of New East Manchester's Strategic Regeneration Framework.

The introduction says: 'East Manchester presents an opportunity for regeneration on a scale and diversity almost unprecedented in an English city.'

Total crime in east Manchester falls 25% in 2000/01 compared to 1999/2000. This includes a 34% reduction in burglary, 26% reduction in vehicle crime and 22% reduction in theft from persons. The figure represents 1,128 fewer crimes. Much of this is a direct result of Operation Excalibur, a high-profile police operation funded by NDC and SRB, which sees more foot patrols, more police horses, mobile police stations and extra police officers cracking down on crime hotspots.

"Crime, that was my forte. I love having a go at the cops. Excalibur was about getting the police out and about. They'd drive round in their cars and vans but never got out. I wasn't having that so, at one of the crime meetings, I told the superintendent straight. Next day the bobbies were out on foot."

Maggie Warburton, Clayton resident.

27th April

"You are the weakest link... goodbye!"

A review day for residents, partners and officers is followed by a social event at Donaheys night club. Hilary Wainwright, academic, writer and editor of *Red Pepper* – who had submerged herself in east Manchester whilst writing her 2003 book, *Reclaim the State: Experiments in Popular Democracy* – is Anne Robinson for the evening as New Deal stages its own version of the popular TV show. The contestants include Baptist minister Tim Presswood and Catholic priest Father Tim. Sean McGonigle and Deputy Chief Executive Steve Mycio represent authority whilst residents Sandra Black and Sheila Rhodes have the audience behind them... and win!

May

The Lord Mayor's Parade.

"Other people had drums or music, we had a chant that Music Stuff had made for us: 'The future's bright, the future's east Manchester!' which we sang as we marched. The day was appalling, it never stopped raining, but the children absolutely loved it. It put us on the map!"

Cath Moran, Senior Regeneration Officer.

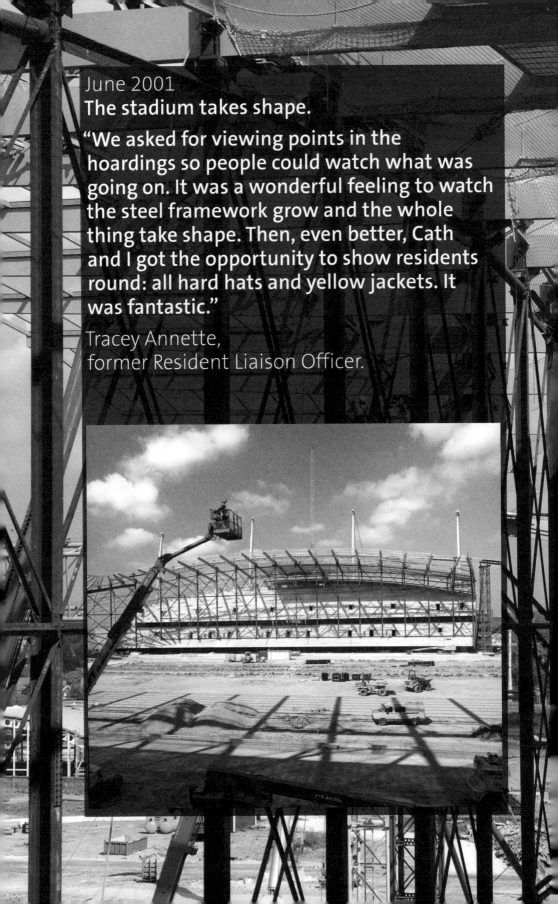

June 2001
The stadium takes shape.

"We asked for viewing points in the hoardings so people could watch what was going on. It was a wonderful feeling to watch the steel framework grow and the whole thing take shape. Then, even better, Cath and I got the opportunity to show residents round: all hard hats and yellow jackets. It was fantastic."

Tracey Annette,
former Resident Liaison Officer.

23rd June

The Wells Centre in Clayton is launched.

Over 800 local people celebrate the launch of their new resource centre. They discover the range of Sure Start services on offer and contribute ideas to further develop the programme. Health visitors, midwives, district nurses, early years' workers, the Family Support Team and a host of volunteers are on hand to share their views and join in the fun.

2001

"There was a competition to come up with the name for our new centre. Lots of ideas came in: I remember the Phoenix Centre was one. Someone suggested the Wells Centre after Mrs Wells who was the oldest resident in Clayton and had lived here all her life. She was delighted to put her name to the building and she cut the ribbon at the opening event."

Debby Crossley, Wells Centre.

"There's nothing more frustrating for these young mothers – who love their babies and want to be good mums – but aren't able to cope. So now with Sure Start [at the Wells Centre] there's always somewhere they can go for a bit of help and advice."

Maggie Warburton, Clayton resident.

"I meet people today who can read and write thanks to the Wells Centre. They were worse than I am – I'm 65 and I still can't write. That needs to be applauded because it's giving people the opportunity to learn."

Bill Booth, Clayton resident.

July

East Manchester Neighbourhood Wardens are launched.

Junior Minister Sally Keeble MP, whose responsibilities include regeneration, launches the new warden service. Janet McGlashen describes their role during a walkabout. (Cont'd on page 76.)

Having stopped work to look after her two children, Debby Crossley was bored and frustrated. New Deal offered new opportunities for residents and Debby took on everything going. Although she didn't realise it at the time, her volunteering helped her to secure a permanent job. Now she's the centre manager for the community centre she helped to set up.

We moved to Clayton when my daughter was just three months old. I was a bit apprehensive at first but it was a nice terraced house — near where the velodrome is now — and the neighbours were supportive.

I joined the local mums and toddlers group and found there were others like me, feeling isolated because there was nothing to do with a youngster. I took time out from work to be with the children — we also had a son by then — but I was bored and wanted to do something stimulating. So when my son started school I did computer courses offered for parents at his primary school.

In 1999 New Deal had just started and was looking for volunteers to help local resident groups. So I did that, which was great, but I still worked part-time as a dinner lady and at B&Q.

Sure Start was set up around that time and, as I wanted to see more services for parents within pram-pushing distance, I volunteered for that too. My first role was to get out there and ask parents what they wanted. With New Deal coming on-stream there were a lot of opportunities so me and another volunteer set up the Ravensbury Tenants' Association and got ourselves invited on to the Beacons board. We'd get people from the Council or from New Deal to come and answer our residents' concerns.

But it all got a bit too much: I was volunteering for New Deal, for Sure Start, running the tenants' association and the community room at the kids' school. I couldn't say no! For the sake of my health, I had to cut back, so I just stayed on the Sure Start board as The Wells Centre was being planned. That was an exciting time: a brand new centre with all the services under one roof and I'd been involved from the very beginning, even helping to decide on a plot of land.

That was the beginning of 2001 and by then I'd started looking out for paid work. Then the receptionist position for the centre was advertised. I didn't think I'd get it because I'd been out of the job market for ten years, and didn't realise that all my volunteering actually counted towards employment. When they told me I'd got the job, I was absolutely over the moon!

Gwen Woollon was brought up in what used to be called Lower Beswick. Her mother worked as a cleaner and her father at the Bradford Pit before becoming a dustbin man. As a girl, an annual highlight was the Whit Week walks when she and her two sisters would have brand new clothes for the community pageant, everyone looking smart for the occasion. She married and brought up four children in the area before moving to London with her second husband after her own children had left home.

After some years in the south she was eager to move back to her Manchester roots and so, in 1995, Gwen and Steve came to Hartwell Close in Beswick – a small private housing development built in 1989 – to view a house that had been repossessed.

I still had loads of friends in the area so was keen to buy something here. The estate was only six years old and because the house had been repossessed, it was fairly cheap. We didn't know at the time that prices were plummeting and everyone here was in negative equity.

When we moved in there were only a couple of empty houses on the close, but slowly it deteriorated. People started selling up and moving out. Private landlords bought up the houses and rented them to, let's say, undesirable families. The young men from one family in particular would use the alleyway at the end of the close as an escape route after putting bricks through windows and making off with TVs and videos. There was soon a 96% crime rate and the police were on the close daily. It just got worse and worse. Within two years 26 out of the 52 properties were empty.

I'd had enough. Something had to be done. I'd heard about New Deal and the money that was coming into the area so Steve and I, and some of the neighbours, went to our first residents' meeting. We weren't expecting much but, to our surprise, they were interested in what we had to say and they listened. We were encouraged to set up a residents' group and apply for funds, which we did. I have to say, New Deal gave us 100% support.

First we got the alleyway blocked off and then had CCTV installed which made a massive difference. We kept attending the crime reduction and housing meetings, applying for funding and gradually getting things done. The crime rate is now less than 1%. There are no empty properties on this close and it's returned to somewhere people want to move to.

For me, that's all about working together. We've never wanted to keep the old terraced properties in this area, but we did want to keep the neighbourhood spirit.

(Cont'd from page 71.)

20 01

"We delayed the launch of the wardens because we felt that the area wasn't ready when we began the Beacons programme. That delay has given us time to work closely with local residents so that we could jointly design, develop and launch a scheme that suited east Manchester."

Paul Cullen, former Community Safety Co-ordinator.

"Once the Cross Tenure Neighbour Nuisance team was working and once we had a strong working relationship with the police, then the climate of the area changed and we were able to introduce the wardens."

Barbara Taylor, Beswick resident.

"Most of the wardens are based locally. They know the families and the problems they face because they may have experienced the same problems."

Jackie Hynes, Community Safety Manager, Eastlands Homes.

16th July

Lord Falconer, Minister for Housing, Planning and Regeneration, tours the area and formally opens the NDC offices.

9th August

Andrew Smith MP, Chief Secretary to the Treasury, visits. He has a particular interest in alleygating and the creation of community gardens so visits several schemes and chats to residents. (See page 143.)

October

The first Very Important Parents Conference is held at the velodrome as part of the Education Action Zone's Neighbourhood Schools Project. Over 500 parents, children and agencies attend. One local dad says, "I want to thank everyone at the Education Action Zone for the difference they have made to mine and my children's lives. I can now help the kids with their homework and my confidence has increased so much, I am going back to college."

(The Conference is repeated successfully for the next four years).

31st January

Launch of EMBRACE (East Manchester Burglary, Robbery and Auto Crime project) aimed at prolific offenders.

"Research suggested that a disproportionate amount of crime was being committed by a relatively small number of offenders. Nowadays, it's accepted there are prolific offenders, but not back then. So, Dave Thompson, the Chief Inspector at Grey Mare Lane, and I presented a plan to the Beacons crime task group. They were 30 residents who met every month to co-ordinate what we were all doing. If they didn't like it, it wouldn't happen. But it made sense to them, they thought it was a good idea, and so EMBRACE came out of that.

"Police officers would work with the Youth Offending Service and the Probation Service and look at all the needs of 20 or so prolific offenders in east Manchester. It wouldn't be just catch-and-convict, it would be about their housing, education and training needs: everything that underpinned their offending. If they wanted to change their ways the team would help them access other Beacons projects. If they didn't, they'd be on their case and quickly apprehended if they re-offended.

"Now Greater Manchester Police is rolling out the Integrated Offender Management Scheme, which has been directly informed by EMBRACE in east Manchester."

Paul Cullen, former Community Safety Co-ordinator.

21st March

The Advertiser free newspaper is launched.

"Back in 1998 there was no free newspaper, certainly no website, community radio, nothing. There was really no way of disseminating information out to the local community. What used to happen, and still does to some extent, is that people would pass on information at the school gates or down the pub. Unfortunately false stories would fly around the area and there wasn't much you could do about it.

"At first a series of glossy newsletters were pushed through everyone's doors, letting them know what we were doing. You've really got to grab people's attention between the doormat and the bin with something like that and so we then produced a newspaper which was supposed to be more 'user-friendly'. But residents knew it was from us and treated it like some kind of propaganda, which I suppose it was.

"What we needed, and what east Manchester needed, was a weekly, local, independent newspaper. So we asked a couple of organisations – including Guardian Media Group – to suggest ideas.

"Local newspapers get nearly all their revenue from advertising, mostly housing advertising. At the time the local economy, and particularly the housing market, was in a bad way so neither of the media groups could make the figures stack up. We asked them if we were to put some money in, could they make it happen. Guardian Media came up with a sliding scale subsidy so that, after five years, the distribution, reputation and advertising revenue would built up sufficiently so they could stand alone.

"The deal is [until 2009] that we'd get two free pages each week for our regeneration information. We give them exclusives, but they are independent so their editorial sometimes challenges the decisions we make. What we did was quite unique. People don't realise it only happened because we made it happen.

"It's a two-way relationship and definitely a win-win situation. What's fascinating is our subsidy should have run up to 2007, but in 2005 they came back to us and said they didn't need it any more as advertising revenue was up and the paper was paying its own way!"

Sean McGonigle.

"Even with the partnership funding from New Deal, we were taking quite a risk. The area was very depressed at the time and we didn't think there'd be enough advertising revenue to ever make it sustainable.

"Editorially, though, it was a brilliant idea. There'd never been a newspaper in east Manchester, and as journalists we knew the area was ripe. There was so much happening with the regeneration effort, it was crying out for a newspaper. We've never had any problems filling the paper with new stories.

"It was absolutely unique, this idea of a newspaper funded by a regeneration agency, but potentially there was a conflict. Although it was agreed we'd be editorially independent, we were initially accused of being in the pocket of our backers. We eventually proved this wasn't the case as we reported on issues that might have been 'uncomfortable' for the regeneration agencies but were still important to our readers.

20
02

21st March

Prime Minister Tony Blair leads the celebrations as the completed City of Manchester Stadium is handed over to the Games' organisers. With Tessa Jowell MP, Secretary of State for Culture Media and Sport, he also meets board representatives, including Barbara Taylor who had brewed up for him in December 1999.

10th June

Resident Maggie Warbuton, Community Safety Co-ordinator Paul Cullen and Sean McGonigle attend a meeting of MPs (those with NDCs in their constituencies) at the House of Commons hosted by John Prescott.

"I said to John Prescott, 'You've not been up to east Manchester, have you? I think it's time you paid us a visit.'

'I will do,' he says.

'You better had,' I says. And he did. And the first person he heard from when he came up was me.

'Do you know Margaret,' he says, 'you're like a breath of fresh air, you tell it like it is, and you don't care who you're talking to.'

'As far as I'm concerned, you're getting paid a wage to do a job and if you're not doing it, I'm going to have a go at you.' We understood each other."

Maggie Warburton, Clayton resident.

15th June

1,000 tickets are distributed free of charge to local resident groups and sports clubs for the Aqua-Pura athletics test event at the stadium.

"We wanted to make sure local people had the opportunity to see the facilities and so we organised regular tours of the site during construction with hard hats and fluorescent jackets. About six weeks before the Games there was a big athletics meeting where we distributed over 1,000 tickets to local groups. Lots of people turned up for that. And then, two nights before it started, we got 1,200 tickets for the opening ceremony dress rehearsal and these went to the households opposite the stadium as a way of recognising the disruption they'd had to put up with. So that was a wonderful opportunity and everyone came along."

Sean McGonigle.

17th June 2002
Asda Wal-Mart opens in east Manchester.

New Deal for Communities was determined that local people would benefit as much as possible from the arrival of the new supermarket. They moved quickly to set up partnerships to ensure residents and jobs were matched.

"Shopping provision in east Manchester was dire. There was a Kwiksave in Beswick district centre — possibly the grimiest in the country and certainly one of the most expensive. Why is it that the most deprived areas always get the most expensive supermarkets? As soon as they heard a superstore was coming they shut up shop and moved out. They were not exactly committed to the area. Thankfully the store was taken over by a local shopkeeper who has kept it going.

"For their weekly shop people had to leave the area and go to Tesco's in Droylsden or Morrisons in Failsworth. It was obvious there was a big gap that needed filling. Not only did we want good quality, affordable shopping, but we were desperate for the jobs that a 180,000 square foot superstore would bring.

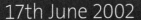

"I wasn't involved in the process of selecting Asda but we were all pleased they'd won the contract. Some of us remembered their store opening in Hulme where they successfully employed dozens of local people. In 2002 they were bought by the American retail giant so the Sportcity store was going to be one of the first – if not the first – Asda Wal-Mart to be built and we wanted as many local people as possible working there.

"Because we already had connections with local agencies we could quickly pull together a partnership between the Employment Service, MANCAT (later The Manchester College) and Asda. The Asda people leading the recruitment were very receptive to our involvement, as we knew they would be, because of the great job they'd done in Hulme.

"When Asda first opened it was like a social club: you'd go to do a bit of shopping and end up chatting to everyone in the place, so it certainly worked in getting local people employed."

Sean McGonigle.

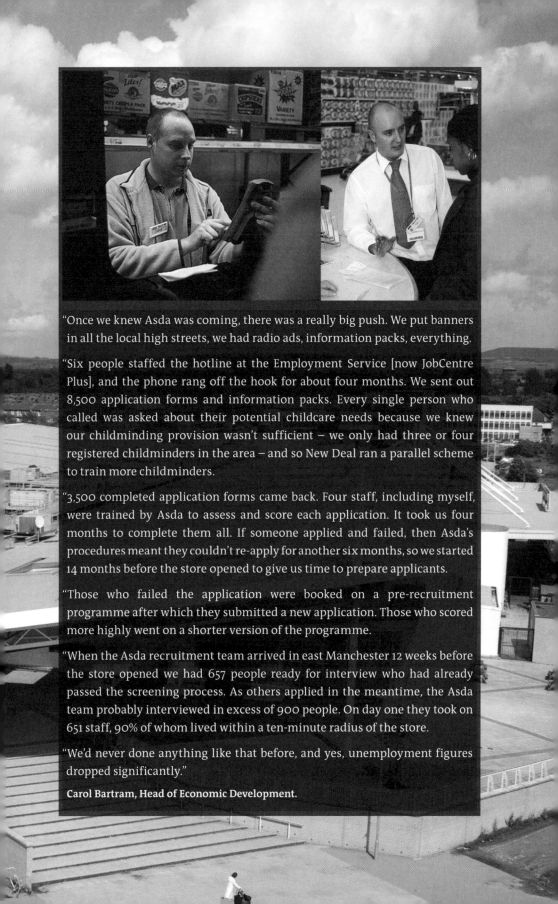

"Once we knew Asda was coming, there was a really big push. We put banners in all the local high streets, we had radio ads, information packs, everything.

"Six people staffed the hotline at the Employment Service [now JobCentre Plus], and the phone rang off the hook for about four months. We sent out 8,500 application forms and information packs. Every single person who called was asked about their potential childcare needs because we knew our childminding provision wasn't sufficient – we only had three or four registered childminders in the area – and so New Deal ran a parallel scheme to train more childminders.

"3,500 completed application forms came back. Four staff, including myself, were trained by Asda to assess and score each application. It took us four months to complete them all. If someone applied and failed, then Asda's procedures meant they couldn't re-apply for another six months, so we started 14 months before the store opened to give us time to prepare applicants.

"Those who failed the application were booked on a pre-recruitment programme after which they submitted a new application. Those who scored more highly went on a shorter version of the programme.

"When the Asda recruitment team arrived in east Manchester 12 weeks before the store opened we had 657 people ready for interview who had already passed the screening process. As others applied in the meantime, the Asda team probably interviewed in excess of 900 people. On day one they took on 651 staff, 90% of whom lived within a ten-minute radius of the store.

"We'd never done anything like that before, and yes, unemployment figures dropped significantly."

Carol Bartram, Head of Economic Development.

For years jobs had been lost in east Manchester as factory after factory closed its gates. In June 2002, hundreds of local people found work at the new Asda Wal-Mart, **Chris Bond** (right) and **Jo-ann Conroy** amongst them.

Chris: I was getting fed up with the late nights working as a stewardess at the British Legion Club and so, when I saw they were building this, I thought I'd give it a go. I hadn't filled in an application form or had an interview for 12 years but it all went well. I got a second interview and they asked me there and then to start in four weeks.

Everyone was very excited when we opened, there hadn't been a shop around here for years. I was brought up in this neighbourhood and remember all the industry: the pit, the wire works, and Francis Shaw's where I used to work when I was younger. I went to school at Philips Park Secondary which was where the car park is now. I sometimes wish my dad could have seen the stadium: he was a big City fan and he'd have loved it.

Asda had only been open a few weeks before the Games and, well, that was absolutely unbelievable. We had people from all over the world walking in here. We used to say "Hello, love," and they were staggered at how friendly we were.

Everything has been good about working here. I've always enjoyed myself. I've met loads of my old school friends, even from when we were only six or seven. They've remembered me and I've recognised them.

Jo-ann: I phoned the number and they sent me an application form and I just took it from there. We were all together for the first interview and for a group task we had to make a presentation on how we'd market a doughnut. A couple of weeks later I was called back for another interview where they offered me the job. I was very excited.

I'd been working in big stores and shops before but I wanted something different, something closer to home. This is only one bus ride away.

We trained in the Longsight and Hyde stores before we came here. On the very first day it was heaving, really busy. We had a DJ playing music and some of us were handing out maps so the customers knew where to go. I was on checkout, and have been on checkout ever since, although now I also help with the self-scan. The customers get to know you, you have your regulars who'll look out for you on the tills. It's fun.

'The client's aspiration was for a high-class sustainable facility that would be economically reliable and a catalyst for regeneration. These aspirations have been met in full and often exceeded, and the City of Manchester Stadium is now considered to be one of the best in Europe.'

From *Manchester: Shaping the City*, RIBA Publications.

18th June

Past, Present and Future is unveiled at the City of Manchester Stadium by Lord Mayor, Councillor Roy Walters.

Offering a welcome from the people of east Manchester, the sculpture was made by local schoolchildren and community groups. Artists Hetty Chapman and Karen Allerton helped too.

12th July

It's National Volunteers' Week and another excuse for a knees-up for residents and staff. This time it's a pub games evening at the Bradford Pub, Beswick with shove ha'penny, skittles, and bar billiards.

July

The Runner by Colin Spofforth is unveiled by former Commonwealth 1,500 metre gold medallist Steve Cram. The nine metre, seven tonne bronze sculpture alongside the Regional Athletics Arena has been commissioned as part of the 'Spirit of Friendship' celebrations.

23rd July

1,200 local Beswick residents attend the dress rehearsal for the Commonwealth Games opening ceremony at the stadium.

2002

"We saw the rehearsals for the opening ceremony. I'll never forget that, it was magical. There was a woman floating from an inflatable globe. Fabulous. My little granddaughter pointed and said, 'Can I have that?' 'Yes,' I said, 'I'll get it for you on the way home'!"

June Webb, Beswick resident.

24th July

Queen's Baton Relay comes along Ashton Old Road and thousands of local residents turn out.

"At the Tameside border there were only half a dozen people watching as the baton went by, but as soon as it crossed into east Manchester there were hundreds lining the route with banners, flags and whistles. Because we'd promoted the event it was absolutely rammed all the way down to the city centre and the road had to be closed. We went along the route giving out 5,000 hand-waving flags... but that wasn't enough!"

John Dwan, former Sport Action Zone Manager.

"Cath and I did ours up in Chorley. I'd have preferred east Manchester but it was still a great day. I remember going out specially to buy training shoes! We only had to run 500 yards but I was worried I couldn't make it, so yes, I had a few practices!"

Tracey Annette, former Resident Liaison Officer.

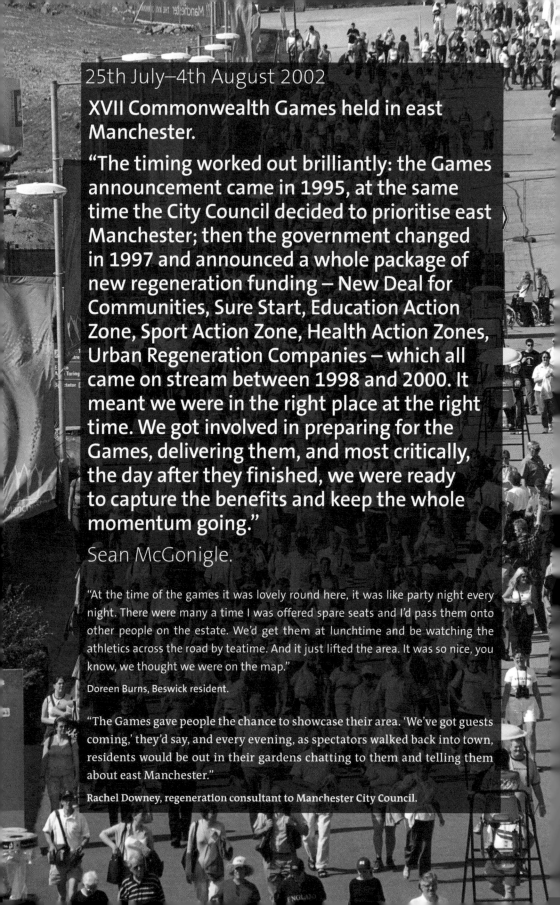

25th July–4th August 2002

XVII Commonwealth Games held in east Manchester.

"The timing worked out brilliantly: the Games announcement came in 1995, at the same time the City Council decided to prioritise east Manchester; then the government changed in 1997 and announced a whole package of new regeneration funding – New Deal for Communities, Sure Start, Education Action Zone, Sport Action Zone, Health Action Zones, Urban Regeneration Companies – which all came on stream between 1998 and 2000. It meant we were in the right place at the right time. We got involved in preparing for the Games, delivering them, and most critically, the day after they finished, we were ready to capture the benefits and keep the whole momentum going."

Sean McGonigle.

"At the time of the games it was lovely round here, it was like party night every night. There were many a time I was offered spare seats and I'd pass them onto other people on the estate. We'd get them at lunchtime and be watching the athletics across the road by teatime. And it just lifted the area. It was so nice, you know, we thought we were on the map."

Doreen Burns, Beswick resident.

"The Games gave people the chance to showcase their area. 'We've got guests coming,' they'd say, and every evening, as spectators walked back into town, residents would be out in their gardens chatting to them and telling them about east Manchester."

Rachel Downey, regeneration consultant to Manchester City Council.

"I was responsible for making sure those on the very edges of society didn't miss out on the opportunities offered by the Games. Starting in 2000, I ran a pre-volunteer programme to encourage people to re-assess their lives.

"I put the feelers out into every possible project, every group, every initiative in east Manchester and made sure they all knew about me and what I was doing. Nothing as big, or as sexy, as the Commonwealth Games was ever going to come to east Manchester again and for many people our programme was their way in. My clients included young people, disabled residents, the unemployed, ethnic minority groups, ex-offenders and those at risk of offending, even active criminals. I was trying to present as many people as possible with hope. Yes, the Games are coming and yes, you can be part of it, but, perhaps more importantly, what do you want to do next?

"I didn't wait for 2002, we set up a course with MANCAT (later The Manchester College) to give people a taste of training. We organised a basic, entry-level course on customer services, health and safety, event management, and team work. We made it as fun as possible and at the end there was a celebration with certificates and Commonwealth Games merchandise as prizes.

"The Games were my way of reaching these groups and that worked brilliantly, but once I'd got their interest, once they were engaged, then the Games had served their purpose and I could focus on helping them to change their lives. I had to bring out the strengths of each individual.

"About 600 people came on the pre-volunteer programme and, although it sounds clichéd now to say it, the positive outcomes were immense. People saw an opportunity and grasped it with both hands. For some it may have been enough for them to reconsider their life's direction, maybe move away from a life of criminality for example, for others it opened doors into training and jobs. The feeling of satisfaction it gives you as a professional worker, well, you just can't put a value on it, it's off the scale. It has to be the most rewarding period of my life."

Heath Cole, former Games Experience Advisor.

"For a long time before, and a long time after, there was a real sense of community that I hadn't seen for a long time. It was good to have it back."

Cath Moran, Senior Regeneration Officer.

"We got it right. A lot of people thought we weren't going to be able to pull it off – it was too big an event – but we did. Everyone was really a part of it and it made everyone proud."

Josie Fletcher, Clayton resident.

VII COMMONWEALTH GAMES

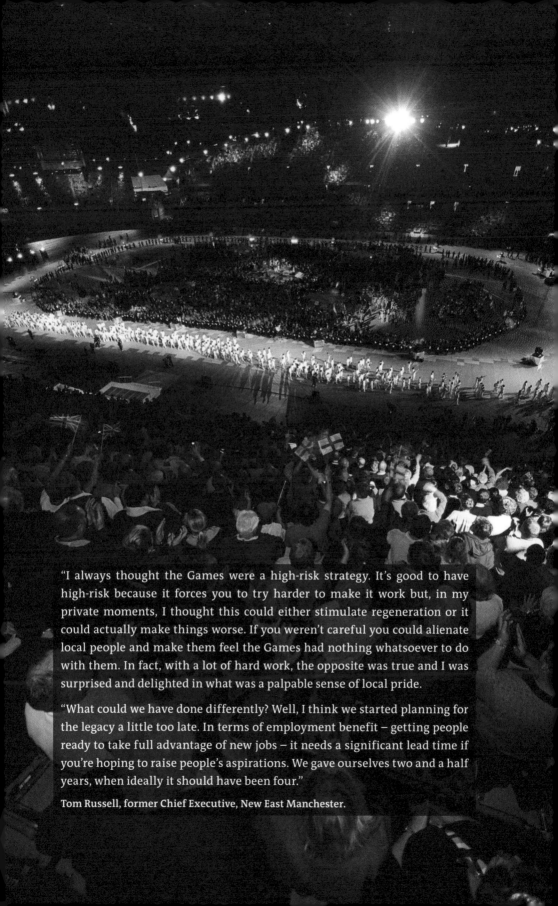

"I always thought the Games were a high-risk strategy. It's good to have high-risk because it forces you to try harder to make it work but, in my private moments, I thought this could either stimulate regeneration or it could actually make things worse. If you weren't careful you could alienate local people and make them feel the Games had nothing whatsoever to do with them. In fact, with a lot of hard work, the opposite was true and I was surprised and delighted in what was a palpable sense of local pride.

"What could we have done differently? Well, I think we started planning for the legacy a little too late. In terms of employment benefit – getting people ready to take full advantage of new jobs – it needs a significant lead time if you're hoping to raise people's aspirations. We gave ourselves two and a half years, when ideally it should have been four."

Tom Russell, former Chief Executive, New East Manchester.

"I can remember I was on my way to meet someone at Asda and everyone was smiling and this lady stopped me and said, 'Erm, can I just ask you, are you from Manchester?' So I said, 'Oh yes, I live local.' So she went, 'I'm a visitor to this city and can I just say it's been absolutely amazing for me. Just make sure everybody knows we really appreciate all that they've put on for us.' I said, 'Where you from?' 'I'm only from Edinburgh,' she went, 'I came to Manchester years ago and I hated it, but I'm here now because my husband insisted we come to the Commonwealth Games. Just make sure everybody knows we appreciate what you've all done for us.' And I went across the road and there were tears rolling down my cheeks, and I

"There were certain sections of the press who were waiting for the Games to fail, for us to fall flat on our faces, but it didn't happen. The opening ceremony was glorious, everything went to plan. It didn't really matter that the weather turned... by then everyone was on a high. Personally it was very hard work, very stressful, but a unique experience. You can understand why people travel the world to work on these events. But also the atmosphere locally was fabulous. We will never see anything like it again. The eyes of the world were on east Manchester for ten days and when it was over, and everyone went home, there was a sense of deflation... a real post-Games hangover."

Sean McGonigle.

Keen on sport as a young girl, Mandy Gilchrest was a championship swimmer by the age of ten. Little did she know that later in life she'd be sharing a stage with world-class athletes right in the heart of her home neighbourhood in east Manchester. Notching up 4,500 hours as a volunteer before, during and after the Commonwealth Games, Mandy became a local celebrity in her own right.

It all started at the end of 2000. My dad signed up to do a volunteering course and before I knew it, he'd put my name down too! There were about 25 of us on that first course and we learnt all about stewarding and how events are organised. Afterwards we worked at different events around the city – a squash tournament or the Chinese New Year parade – to gain experience. Once the stadium was ready I moved into the visitor centre before doing ticket sales.

The Games were getting closer and closer and we applied for different volunteering posts. I was also nominated by about 1,000 people around east Manchester to be one of the bearers in the Queen's Baton Relay the day before the Games. I was in floods of tears that day... it was such an emotional experience. It felt like I'd been carrying it for ages but it was only for a short time. Even now that doesn't seem real.

The next day I went to the stadium and found out I'd been chosen as a medal bearer! A medal bearer! I couldn't believe it. I was the first disabled person to be selected to carry medals into the stadium. The very first one I did was an England gold – for javelin, I think – and the stadium was absolutely electrifying. My chair was shaking! I thought I was going to take off and start flying around!

I gave out so many. I remember one day, the Countess of Wessex came into the tunnel where we were waiting. We were supposed to call her 'Your Royal Highness' but she came up to me and said, "Hello Mandy," and I so I said, "Hello Sophie," and we had a good chat. But I'm thinking, "This is not normal. I'm just Mandy from Clayton. What am I doing talking to royalty!"

It's a shame it all had to end, but it made such a difference. It gave me the confidence to turn my life around. It opened lot of doors and I can honestly say it's changed my life and made me much happier.

27–28th July

During the Games...

First 'Parties in the Park' are at Philips and Delamere Parks on the first weekend of the Games. The fun is repeated in Bradford and Openshaw Parks the following weekend. £50,000 comes from the Commonwealth Games 'pot' for local people to celebrate this amazing event on their doorsteps.

"Food was subsidised, fairground rides were free, we had a stage, hired brass bands, teddy bears' picnic, we did everything."

Cath Moran, Senior Regeneration Officer.

"It was a great event, a beautiful day. We had thousands of people down there: as well as local people enjoying themselves, there were lots of spectators here for the Games who were wandering between venues and got involved. People just wanted to be a part of it."

Josie Fletcher, Clayton resident.

29th July

HRH Duke of Kent visits the Wells Centre in Clayton and meets Mrs Wells, Clayton's oldest resident and the community centre's namesake.

31st July

HRH Earl and Countess of Wessex (Edward and Sophie) open the Grange Community Resource Centre in Beswick.

July–August

Keeping the kids busy...

During the summer of 2002, the Beacons area receives extra funding from the Home Office and Youth Justice Board as part of their Splash and Splash Extra initiatives which aim to divert children and young people away from crime.

To add to the annual summer play schemes organised by JOG (Joint Openshaw Group, a community group), the Youth Service and others organise activities from go-karting to martial arts.

(Figures later show total crime fell by 7.4% between June and August. So, it worked and was repeated in 2003.)

July

Aspire is launched.

"Aspire evolved from consultations with local businesses and the analysis of their recruitment patterns. A significant number of employers in the area were manufacturers and, for some, there were only particular times of the year when their lines were at a peak production. We mapped this across a large number of local companies and looked for a solution that would support local companies as well as address the cycle of residents signing on and off benefits as and when work became available. We looked at a range of projects nationally and formed a strong partnership with Hull Joblink who operated a small Jobshare programme with eight manufacturers.

"The result was Aspire, the east Manchester not-for-profit recruitment agency, which employed staff on a twelve-month contract and 'shared' them with employers as they needed them.

"Aspire has now evolved into the Manchester Apprenticeship Company which has employed significant numbers of apprentices displaced due to the recession. The apprentices are moved around from company to company, but they remain in full-time employment and get to complete their qualifications. It works really well."

Carol Bartram, Head of Economic Development.

August

Learning4U prospectus launched at the Grange by Council Leader, Richard Leese.

The prospectus lists all the courses and centres locally where residents can continue learning. There are courses for fun and for work; there are profiles of other residents who have already moved onto greater things; and there's an advice line (linked to advisors at Step Ahead, the local employment centre) for those who need guidance.

August

For the first time the Beacons area enters the North West Britain in Bloom competition and wins an award in the 'Best Space in Community Housing' category.

The winning area stretches from Rylance Street, through Beswick and into Openshaw where green-fingered residents have spruced up their hanging baskets, community centres, parks, community gardens and play spaces.

Susan Young, winner of the overall best garden, says, "The competition was fantastic. I was very happy to win a prize – it makes all the effort worthwhile."

6th August

RoadPeace Memorial Garden officially opens at the Grange.

Two years on from the tragic deaths of friends Jodie Webb and Joanne Greenwood – killed as innocent passengers of a dangerous driver on Jodie's 21st birthday – the young women's families celebrate the opening of the RoadPeace Garden.

Inspired by Jodie's mother, June, the garden has been developed by Groundwork and will be used as part of a local road safety campaign to raise the profile of dangerous driving and its consequences.

June Webb (left) and June Greenwood

"There was one particular day which was a turning point for me: I was either going to give up totally or I was going to fight back. I phoned RoadPeace. They'd been in the same situation as us and they gave me the strength to carry on. So I decided to fight back.

"We never thought we'd get a memorial garden, never thought it was possible. Yes, we wanted a memorial to Jodie and Joanne, but I also wanted to educate the younger ones. The next generation of drivers have to realise that these were needless deaths. We went to see New Deal and they put the wheels in motion and we got our RoadPeace Garden."

June Webb, Beswick resident.

Carol Littlewood is an inspiration to everyone she advises. During a lengthy illness she thought she might never work again but, with the help of New Deal for Communities, she gradually returned to the workplace. Now she helps others to do the same.

It wasn't the first time I'd been off work. But this time – back in 1998 – it was due to physical problems with my back, my knees and my hips which meant I couldn't go on. I used to pack flowers in a warehouse and it was demanding work but I had to stop.

While I was on long-term sick a woman from Stepping Stones introduced herself at the health centre. By then I'd been off for six years and was thinking I was ready to get back to work. This woman got me onto a basic IT course for people who'd never sat in front of a computer screen before.

At about that time I got chatting with Elaine Wright, who arranged for me to do some volunteering at New Deal's offices, stuffing envelopes for the post on Friday afternoons. My confidence was rock bottom at that point but it was great, everyone was very friendly which made it much easier for me.

After a few months of volunteering, I started to apply for jobs as they came up. I went for the Regeneration Assistants Programme [see page 120] and for the Guidance Promotion Worker position at Work Solutions. I didn't get the Assistant job but I did get to become a Guidance Promotion Worker.

We worked outreach in the old Gorton Market where we'd give people advice on their work options. Because I'd been there – on their side of the fence if you like – I was in a better position to help. From thinking there was no hope for me, here I was, working again, this time in something that didn't involve hard physical effort. I still had panic attacks and depression and still do, but they are controlled. Coming out to work has made it ten times better.

I was put through an NVQ Level 3 in Information, Advice and Guidance and that was really scary! I didn't think I could do it, was continually doubting myself, but took it in stages and passed! I was then promoted to Employment and Training Consultant and have since completed my Level 4. For part of each week I also work on a Helping Hands pilot scheme where we look at all the barriers that keep people away from the workplace – childcare, housing, debts – and we try to help them over the long term.

So, yes, I love my work, and I do a good job, even though I say so myself!

28th September

Prime Minister Tony Blair and Deputy Prime Minister John Prescott visit east Manchester. They meet the six Resident Board Representatives as well as two previous Board Representatives whom Tony Blair had met back in 1999. They then go on to open the newly improved Bradford Park, opposite the Grange Community Centre.

> "People can see change happening here and there is still a fantastic amount to do. But don't let anyone tell you there is not real change in areas like this. We are providing the resources but it is local people providing the energy."
>
> **Prime Minister Tony Blair.**

25th October

The drug misusers support project Outlook is launched providing activities, training, counselling, and ultimately employment support. It's all about developing skills, confidence, self-esteem and motivation. (See page 108.)

13th December

Ballot result announcement for the stock transfer of 207 properties in Higher Openshaw to Mosscare Housing.

December

Active Dads.

The breakfast session at one primary school attracts over 20 dads, brothers and granddads. One father of six on the project said, "My son now comes with me to walk the dog. We never really talked before because there were always other people around but now he's much better behaved."

1st January

Howard Bernstein, Chief Executive, Manchester City Council is knighted for services to the reconstruction of Manchester and the XVII Commonwealth Games.

January

Groundwork, NDC and their partners celebrate as the Community Environment Programme wins a BURA (British Urban Regeneration Association) Award for Outstanding Contribution to Regeneration. According to the panel the main lesson of the programme is that 'enabling fractured and damaged communities to be self-sufficient requires revenue streams that fund community workers to support local people over a number of years. It takes time to understand the needs of an area and to develop the skills and talents of local people. When building sustainable communities quick fixes are just not an option.'

April

East Manchester Consortium comes on-stream.

"The Consortium was our attempt at bringing the larger voluntary agencies together and encouraging them to work collaboratively. But it was difficult from day one. There were, at times, elements of mistrust between some groups in the east Manchester voluntary sector which we weren't able to overcome at first. So the Consortium as a network didn't work as well as we'd hoped: many didn't have the time to come together for what was perceived to be a 'talking shop'; most were, understandably, more interested in getting on and doing their own thing.

"But the Consortium was good at providing training, at capacity building and at running the East Manchester Grants Partnership. The training project offered hours and hours of quality training – much of it provided in partnership with Manchester Adult Education Service – which gave many residents a route into more formal education and, ultimately, jobs.

"The Grants Partnership was about putting residents in control. A panel of residents involved in local voluntary groups would assess bids from other voluntary groups – play schemes, church groups, friends of parks – and award small grants. It wasn't a huge pot of money – they had a budget of £15,000 a year – but that wasn't important, it was more about bringing people together. The Partnership allowed people to look outside their own box and the Consortium eventually made the larger groups examine their own motives and make positive changes."

Philip Bradley, Principal Regeneration Officer.

In 2001, New Deal for Communities helped establish Outlook, a free, non-judgmental and confidential service to those with drug problems. Mike McCarrick is one of their many success stories.

I started using heroin when I was 22 or 23. I guess it was down to peer pressure. There were some fairly intimidating people around at the time and it was hard to say no. Looking back, I suppose I was quite naive and vulnerable.

It got pretty bad. I was spending £100–130 a day on drugs and yes, I turned to crime to pay for my habit. Initially it was shoplifting and then I'd go and rip copper pipes and boilers out of derelict houses and sell them for scrap. Until I was caught and charged I didn't realise that was as serious as burglary. I was given a Drug Treatment and Testing Order, which is an alternative to going to prison. It was a second chance, a chance to address the problem.

When I first came to Outlook I was using maybe once or twice a week, but also taking the heroin substitute, methodone. You have to be able to show you are serious about getting off drugs, you have to be making an effort. I'd come every day and stay all day, from morning till night. It's important to stay away from your usual places and associates. At Outlook it felt good to be accepted, amongst people tackling the same issues. I no longer felt excluded.

We'd do group therapy, one-to-one therapy, personal development, art and music. There's an internet café, and you can even have a massage. After about twelve months I was encouraged to go into detox to come off the heroin and the methodone. I'd tried to detox before, on my own, but never had the follow-up support. This time everything was in place: once I'd detoxed I was going to start a college course.

As part of an NVQ Level 2 in Health and Social Care at The Manchester College I came back to Outlook to do the placement part of the course and am now doing my Level 3. I'm also on Outlook's Member Graduate Scheme which gives a solid foundation from which to go out there and find work. There's more to this than just getting clean and Outlook understand that.

Now I'm living in a new area and I've made contact again with my family who live locally. It's taken a while for the trust to be rebuilt. After 12 years on heroin, they needed to know I was going to stay clean this time. It's a big weight off my mother's shoulders.

April

The Beacons Women's Network is set up to encourage women who don't normally get involved in community activities; to use assertive and articulate women as positive role models; and to promote a greater sense of integration.

"For the first time women from different cultures were brought together and despite language difficulties we were all able to make ourselves understood.

"I went to Rainbow Haven [the refugee and asylum-seeker drop-in] and encouraged some of the ladies from there to come and join us. For them it was an eye-opener, it showed them how other women lived. Because we provided childcare they were able to bring their children and so, for a couple of hours each month, they could do something special for themselves.

Some of the Women's Network with their Northern Irish guests

"Every month was different. We laid on trips; we had belly-dancing; card-making workshops; baking sessions; in the summer we had barbecues. We even brought three women over from Belfast who told us what life was like for them... that was very interesting. The asylum-seekers from Rainbow Haven had been through some of that themselves."

Sandra Black, Beswick resident and Project Co-ordinator.

8th and 9th April

Regeneration is put under the spotlight with a conference at Manchester Town Hall put on by NDC staff and residents attended by more than 120 people.

Regeneration professionals come from far and wide to attend this 'East Manchester Presents...' conference. Residents and officers share their experiences with best practice presentations, bus tours and more than 20 workshops. *Seeing it for Real*, a video made by residents, showcases progress.

"I was asked to make a little speech about how the regeneration had affected the area and, at the end, I gave this illustration of how things had changed. I used to have a German shepherd called Bruce. He was bought as a guard dog, because we had our fair share of trouble in those days, and he did his job well. When he passed away, I decided to replace him. By then the area had improved so much I felt I no longer needed a guard dog and so I now have Jack, a Labrador who's a big softy and a great companion."

Hedley Carter, Chariot Office Supplies and Beacons Board Member.

30th April

Voting closes for the stock transfer of 2,822 council homes to Eastlands Homes. The ballot results in a 90% 'Yes' vote in favour of the transfer, based on a 76% turnout. Eastlands Homes is established in September (see page 115).

"Most of our properties had a negative market value and needed a lot spending on them to bring them up to a decent standard. A funding mechanism was required that gave a sort of dowry, so the new owners of the stock – whether it was a local housing company or an existing housing association – could then borrow against future rents. The Estates Renewal Challenge Fund – which we didn't get – was exactly that mechanism for giving a grant that covered the negative valuation.

"Initially the Government had said none of the £77 million coming to east Manchester through NDC and SRB could be spent on housing. Education, crime prevention, health and dealing with worklessness, were to be the priorities. But we were adamant that the area's problems could not be tackled effectively if housing was left out. The condition of people's homes was fundamental to everything else. Whitehall finally agreed and, in the end, about £35 million of that total was spent on sorting out the housing issue. [£23 million went to set up Eastlands Homes; the rest was spent on demolitions and facelifting some private sector housing.]

"Interestingly there were no complaints that such a large proportion of our 'win' was spent on council housing considering they made up only a third of the total housing stock. I think people realised that improvements to council houses would have a knock-on effect on the whole area. Yes, there were massive problems with privately owned houses, especially where they were rented, but no-one could move on until the council properties were sorted.

"I never imagined it wouldn't be approved. We'd done a lot of work, particularly with the residents' and tenants' groups, explaining the benefits. We'd made sure all council tenants knew what the transfer was about, what the benefits would be and what it would mean for them so they could make an informed decision. Over half of eligible tenants had to vote yes for the transfer to be approved. In the end 90% said yes and it's been a huge success since then on so many levels. It meant Eastlands was able to immediately start improving people's houses. There have been new kitchens, bathrooms, doors, windows, heating systems, re-wiring, roofs, boundary treatments. Everyone had at least one improvement in the first couple of years and many have had several. Now the demand for social housing has massively improved in east Manchester. There are very long waiting lists when, ten years ago, no-one wanted to live here."

Sean McGonigle.

"When she started to explain what stock transfer was, we all sat there looking at her as if she had two heads and was speaking a foreign language... we hadn't a clue! But then we had another meeting, and another, and so it started to make sense.

"They asked us to form a steering group, which we did, but we insisted that, as well as council tenants, it must include people who had bought their council houses. The 'right-to-buys' had lived through all the bad times and they were as keen as anyone to see the place turn around. So then it got serious. We needed an independent tenants' advisor and we were not going to take one that the town hall allocated, so we recruited our own. They were brilliant, they really got on board with us and helped us through the process.

"Many other stock transfers at that time were moving council housing to existing housing associations, but the steering committee and the shadow board – that we'd also had to set up – decided we'd form a totally new company to manage east Manchester's social housing. So we came up with the name and set up Eastlands Homes."

Linda Wagner, Beswick resident.

11th May
Manchester City's last game at Maine Road in Moss Side. They lose to Southampton 0–1.

June
Refugee and Asylum Seeker drop-in pilots.

"We were considering two different models of support. The first was very much an informal social opportunity, a cup of tea and a chat, and the other was more of a sign-posting facility where outreach workers were on hand to offer advice and support. We wanted to find out which approach was more appropriate. Not surprisingly, the answer was a bit of both: a socialising network with some targetted support. So with that format we helped set up Rainbow Haven which continues to provide a friendly welcome to this day."

Philip Bradley, Principal Regeneration Officer.

June
The New York Times runs an article about Eastserve, writing that 'in Manchester, the once-grimy Victorian city famous as the birthplace of the Industrial Revolution, Wi-Fi is being used, for the first time ever on this scale, as a way to bridge the digital divide.'

8th July
Handover of City of Manchester Stadium to Manchester City FC.

Almost as soon as the Games left Manchester in 2002 work started on converting the stadium. The running track was dug up to be re-laid at other venues and the ground level was lowered so an additional tier of 12,000 seats could be added to increase the capacity to 47,726. The North Stand, which had been a temporary structure for the duration of the Games, was constructed to complete the stadium.

Under an agreement between Manchester City Council and MCFC, 50% of the value of every seat over 32,000 and 60% of the value of every seat above 40,000 sold at future City matches will be reinvested into sporting facilities and projects in the east Manchester area. (Approximately £2 million of revenue is subsequently generated annually from these and other sources.)

"There was indignant fury from the likes of Jonathan Edwards [world champion triple jumper] and Sebastian Coe when the track was ripped up but it was pointless: no-one was going to reuse a 36,000-seater athletics stadium at anything like its full capacity. As far as I can remember there was always the expectation that City was going to take on the stadium after the Games. Maine Road was over 80 years old and the crowds, amongst all those terraced houses in Moss Side, were difficult to manage.

"This stadium is close to the city centre and easily accessible to motorways. The residents, although they were close, weren't right on top of it like at Maine Road. Most local people were supportive of the club moving over here. The job opportunities alone were a big boost: the shops and pubs have done well out of it and there have been plenty of part-time jobs in catering, security and stewarding. It's been really important."

Sean McGonigle.

"There was a lot of opposition from the residents at first. I think it was fear of the unknown. They said, 'Oh, it'll be awful, we won't be able to get out of the estate with all the parked cars; there'll be rubbish everywhere.' But I took the view that we'd been given a voice, so let's use it. We did get involved, and we were consulted. So we now have parking permits that work wonderfully. The litter is always cleared away. Match days are no problem here."

Doreen Burns, Beswick resident.

Residents Bill Booth, Elaine Wright and Sandra Black meet City manager, Kevin Keegan

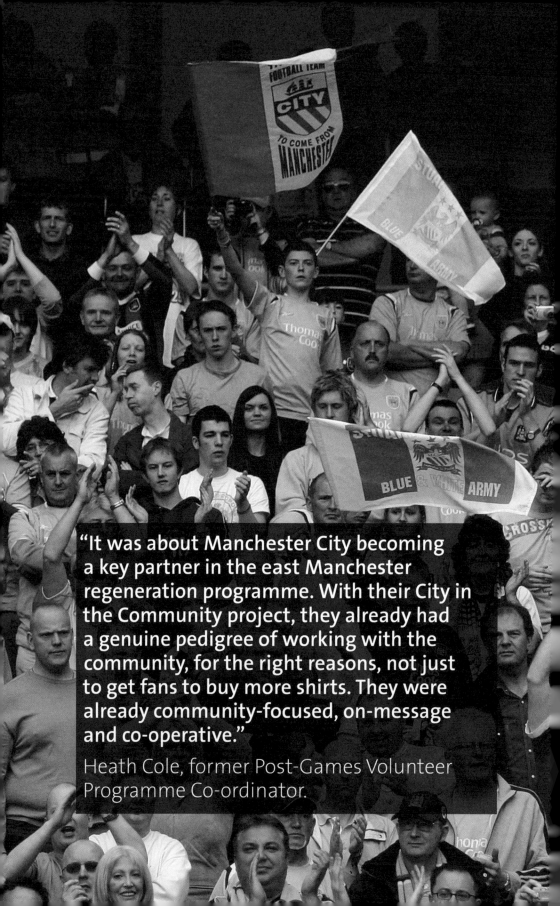

"It was about Manchester City becoming a key partner in the east Manchester regeneration programme. With their City in the Community project, they already had a genuine pedigree of working with the community, for the right reasons, not just to get fans to buy more shirts. They were already community-focused, on-message and co-operative."

Heath Cole, former Post-Games Volunteer Programme Co-ordinator.

22nd August

Step Ahead 2 in Openshaw – the employment and training support office – is opened by Manchester City's Jon Macken.

11th September

Eastlands Homes is launched.

Following the ballot in April, the newly formed housing association gets up and running. £23 million of the Beacons £77 million 'pot' goes towards paying for the transfer of council houses to Eastlands Homes. A significant programme of investment can now start which will bring homes up to the Government's Decent Homes Standard by 2010. The 15-strong management board includes five tenants and one resident representative.

12th September

Citizens Advice Bureau Plus is officially opened by Tony Lloyd MP.

Another partnership success: Citizens Advice, Jobcentre Plus, the Pension Service, Manchester Advice and Age Concern all get together for this one. Rather than part-time, the new service is now open five days a week. (In its first month it dealt with four times its usual number of appointments and 400 residents got in touch).

September

"In our most deprived areas – chosen because they have the worst poverty, the highest unemployment and the lowest educational achievement – we created the New Deal and Neighbourhood Renewal Programmes – £4 billion worth of investment. And in every single one of those New Deal areas unemployment, crime and poverty levels have fallen, and education standards have risen."

John Prescott, Deputy Prime Minister, to the 2003 Labour Party conference in Bournemouth.

3rd October

Sausage Sarnies.

The Beswick Community Café at the Church of the Resurrection serve up locally produced Riley's sausages as part of their Manchester Food and Drink Festival celebrations.

(There's fresh fruit as pudding.)

October 2004

First phase £125 million of Housing Market Renewal money is announced.

'Plans for the biggest housing regeneration project in Britain for more than 30 years were approved yesterday in an attempt to revive twin cities blighted by abandoned neighbourhoods and collapsing property markets.

The government allocated £125 million for a two-and-a-half-year programme in Manchester and Salford to demolish old houses and build new ones. Hundreds of millions of pounds could follow in partnerships with developers involving new schools and shopping centres.

While several thousand houses could eventually face demolition, one of the project leaders, Eamonn Boylan, the deputy chief executive of Manchester City Council, insisted last night: "This is not a return to wholesale slum clearance, a scorched earth policy. We aim to revive the marketplace and provide higher quality homes for the existing community."'

Peter Hetherington, *The Guardian*, 7th October.

18th November

Another BURA award. This time Sportcity with the Ashton Canal is the winner for Outstanding Contribution to Regeneration.

19th November

New Police Chief Constable Mike Todd visits east Manchester and meets residents.

January

Olivia Lodge opens.

It's a residential centre for young mums with life skills training and a crèche. Beacons' money pays for community facilities such as the meeting room and laundrette, which are shared with local groups.

> "We set ourselves some ambitious targets and Olivia Lodge was one of them. There was a need for some kind of supported housing, foyer-type facility where young mums would have somewhere to live but also get parenting support and advice on jobs and training. Olivia Lodge was one of our successes."
>
> **Libby Graham, Director of Social Programmes.**

20th January

Manchester Regional Athletics Arena opens.

The Commonwealth Games warm-up track is transformed into a £3.5 million 6,500-seat athletics arena with eight 400-metre lanes.

Samaya Keane was just 12 years old when New Deal for Communities was established. A self-confessed tearaway, Samaya – or 'Kippa' as she is better known – was already well known to the police. Abandoned and derelict houses in her neighbourhood of Higher Openshaw were her playground.

New Deal has funded sports development work through the Sport Action Zone, the Nacro Sports Project and Manchester Leisure. Sports activity in the evenings, weekends and through school holidays was provided and – such is her love of football – Kippa got involved in everything on offer.

With the support of outreach youth workers, she diverted her energies into football and encouraged others in her area. She's since collected awards at the Houses of Parliament and given eloquent speeches about the role of community sport to audiences including the police officers who apprehended her years earlier.

We used to smash up empty properties, burn out derelict houses. Yes, I was well naughty when I was a kid. There was nothing for us to do, so we'd have to entertain ourselves. The place was really run down and I remember there was one row of terraced houses where we smashed holes in all the inside walls. When the police came to try and catch us, we'd run in one side, through all the holes we'd made and out the other side.

But I did get caught, loads of times, and the police told me that if I didn't change my ways, I'd be taken off my mum. They said I was a danger to myself and to the public.

That's when I started to take football seriously. I'd always hung out with the lads, never with the girls, and we used to play at St Gregory's in Openshaw, where Sporting Edge is now. I had a passion for football and was a lot better than many of the boys, and they didn't like that! The sports development worker invited Manchester City to come and see me and they signed me there and then for their under-12s girls' team.

There were leagues all over east Manchester. John Dwan [Sport Action Zone Manager at New Deal] set up tournaments between teams in Beswick, Ancoats or Newton Heath: we played all over. We got involved with Nacro and Groundwork, all of them working with the kids, giving them something to do.

I didn't do any of my GCSEs at school. I was still very naughty at school and was often sent home, but they never actually threw me out. I went on to do a BTEC National and now I'm doing a foundation degree in sports coaching at The Manchester College. No-one else round here has gone on to higher education.

2nd February

2004

John Prescott MP visits east Manchester and goes first to Ravensbury Primary School in Clayton. He then meets Diane Vickers at her home and she shows him round the Stuart Street community garden. He is so impressed with the garden he later mentions it in a number of speeches. Diane has a sweep with her colleagues and neighbours about which biscuit Prescott will eat – unseen by her he takes a digestive and slips it into his pocket. Diane is interviewed twice about the biscuits on Radio Manchester.

"That visit gave us so much credibility. It was a real feather in our cap."

Diane Vickers, Clayton resident.

14th February

Sarah Armitt, Nick Buckley, Susan Robinson and Gina Twigg become the first cohort on the Regeneration Assistants Project. Local residents are employed for two years and led through an accredited training programme combined with work-based experience designed for a career in regeneration. (See page 140.)

26th February

Launch of East Manchester Landlord Information Service at the City of Manchester Stadium.

Private and social landlords can now check a database that will help prevent antisocial tenants moving around the area unchallenged.

3rd March

Launch of new Beacons website at the City of Manchester Stadium.

There's a newsroom where residents can read about the latest activities and a media gallery with photos and video clips made by local people.

Already, by 2004, 1336 private sector houses have been improved, many with new boundary treatments and 'facelifts'.
Source: System K Lifetime Outputs.

May

Beswick resident Danny Robinson, 13, attends a consultation meeting with his school at the City of Manchester Stadium. "There were lots of regeneration people and council officials there. The only way I can put it is that I blabbered on for an hour and a half about the parks and services to schools."

20
04

> "Danny was unique because he was the first young person to independently articulate the shortcomings in his area – the issues around his park – which better informed our own efforts."
>
> **Philip Bradley, Senior Regeneration Officer.**

(He later becomes one of the first Young Advisors, see page 136, and a leading light in the development of the Bang of the Voice youth forum).

12th May

The Trouble with Being Lee is broadcast as part of the BBC's *One Life* series.

For four months the BBC followed the fortunes of the prolific offender programme, EMBRACE, demonstrating how PC Lance Thomas and his partners helped young people keep on the straight and narrow.

> "Lee had been identified by his youth offending team as a risk to the community. But since PC Thomas began keeping a closer eye on Lee as part of EMBRACE – picking him up whenever he was loitering with a bad crowd, drilling into him the consequences of committing another offence – Lee seemed to turn a corner. He stopped taking drugs, almost stopped drinking vodka, and kept a clean sheet. When it came to the judge having to pass sentence for Lee's earlier car theft, he decided Lee had responded well enough to the EMBRACE project to be spared a custodial sentence. By the time the film crew had packed its bags and left Openshaw, Lee had been crime-free for nearly a year."
>
> **Joe Joseph, *The Times*.**

13th June

The central core of *B of the Bang* arrives in Manchester. It's the largest load that could be transferred via road from the factory in Sheffield.

2004

18th June
Red Hot Chili Peppers and James Brown stage the first ever concert at the City of Manchester Stadium.

538 new jobs have been created so far that can be directly attributed to the New Deal for Communities programme (This doesn't include the hundreds of jobs at employers like Asda that NDC have had a hand in; see page 80).
Source: System K Lifetime Outputs.

26th July
Secretary of State for Transport Alistair Darling MP declines to approve extension plans for the Metrolink which would have brought trams gliding into east Manchester.

July–August
Over 500 local schoolchildren enjoy a total of 70,000 hours of activities laid on for them across east Manchester... that's about three and a half weeks each!

"... I was working on summer play schemes at the time and, together with the Youth Service, we met with Danny Robinson (see page 121), and came up with the Multi-Agency Parks Project to encourage local residents to 'reclaim' their parks and to make them safer places to play. We organised events in four parks and had up to 100 children each night for six weeks. The city-wide 'Parktastic' project, which runs all year round, comes directly from the success we had in east Manchester."

Jeff Burns, Community Development Manager.

8th September
The samba band Bloco Novo is born.

After outreach workshops in the local parks the band, such as it is, makes its debut appearance at The John Gilmore Centre in Clayton. Three of the five-strong audience join the band! (Under the leadership of Zac Sargent, and with support from the Arts and Culture Team, the band has since performed all over the North West).

10th September
Social Inclusion Toolkit is unveiled at the Grange.

"The Toolkit helped service providers reach a wider range of local residents. By following the 'top tips' services could challenge the social exclusion experienced by some and create more socially inclusive opportunities for all."

Philip Bradley, Principal Regeneration Officer.

13th September

Ashbury Meadow Primary School opens, supported by £250,000 from NDC.

"When I became head in 2003 the two schools – Ashbury Primary and Bank Meadow Primary – merged into Ashbury Meadow but were still on two sites. It wasn't until the Autumn term of 2004 that we all moved into this new building. The old schools were both in need of repair and were no longer viable individually. Their intakes had shrunk and neither was working to capacity, so it made sense to put them together.

"Building a new school here sent a strong message out to the community: 'We believe in you,' we were saying, 'we know you are worth it'. At the new school we've now got a much better environment and facilities. Our ICT suite, play and sport facilities are all vastly improved. The central courtyard is a valuable resource: a safe, quiet area where children even grow their own fruit and vegetables.

"Having the children's centre incorporated into the school has made an enormous difference. Parents can get involved in work-related training courses from confidence-building to improving numeracy and literacy. There's relaxation for pregnant mums, baby massage, and a whole gamut of activities that the parents and children can do together.

"I believe one of the keys to children's education is being able to involve the parents. School is viewed with suspicion by some parents, perhaps because they haven't had a good experience themselves, so any non-threatening activities that the parents and children can share at school are incredibly useful."

Lorna Rushton, Head Teacher.

"I hope the staff feel more valued now. They seem to enjoy their work more and I think this has a knock-on effect with the children and the parents. If the teachers are happy, the children will be happy and more receptive to learning."

Irene Johnson, Beswick resident.

Education has been a priority for New Deal for Communities since the very beginning of its programme. In 2000 east Manchester became an Education Action Zone and every school in the area has benefited from additional investment. Here, local residents **Amanda Ward** (right) and **Tracey Haselden** recount their journeys to becoming Teaching Assistants at Ashbury Meadow Primary School.

Amanda: As my children were at nursery I enrolled on a course there about learning through play and that, I suppose, is how it all started for me. I then became a lunchtime organiser at the old Ashbury's School and for a couple of mornings a week I'd go to the Manchester Settlement — when they were still on Bosworth Street in Beswick — and do my NVQ Level 2 in Childcare and Early Education.

At the time the deputy at the old school had some funding for early literacy support and he offered me a job, and that's how I got into full-time work.

Tracey: I used to go to a mother and toddler group when my kids were little and I knew then, I just knew, that I wanted to work with young children. I went to college full-time for two years and did a BTEC Level 3 in Nursery Nursing and Childcare. When I left college, the Education Action Zone were advertising for Teaching Assistants. I didn't get the first job I went for — it would have been split over two schools — but then I was offered a full-time job at Bank Meadow, which I took.

Amanda: Since I've been here I've gone on to do Level 3 and we've had so much training through work, I just can't remember all the courses.

Tracey: I think we must have done everything there is to do about professional development and working with children.

Amanda: It's been good for us and the children that we are both from the local area. The children like the idea that we live in Beswick. We've had the same upbringing as them, we're on the same wavelength as most of their parents. It's nice to be able to give something back to the community that's brought you up, that's what I like about working here.

Tracey: Some of the parents see us as more approachable. But yes, we've both benefited from all this regeneration. Back then I thought I was wasting my time working — that financially it wasn't worth it — but I wouldn't go back on benefits again, I couldn't. My daughter's at college now, doing childcare. I'd like her to go on to university and maybe become a teacher, do something better than me anyway.

22nd September

Launch of Beacons 'No Accident' road safety video at The Printworks.

Following June Webb's campaign for the RoadPeace Memorial Garden (see page 103), a video is produced locally to promote road safety.

(In October 2009, June becomes one of five finalists for the People's Award at the National Justice Awards).

15th November

With the Lord Mayor's help, children from St Brigid's RC Primary School, CofE School of The Resurrection, and Ravensbury Community School insert a time capsule into one of *B of the Bang's* 180 spikes.

12th January

B of the Bang is officially launched.

Inspired by sprinter Linford Christie's claim that he started his races on the 'b of the bang', the sculpture is the tallest in Britain. Designed by Thomas Heatherwick Studio, it has been commissioned to commemorate the 2002 Commonwealth Games.

17th January

The Grange in Beswick becomes a locally managed community centre run by 4CT. (See page 129.)

(See page 129.)

"The best thing we've done is take over the Grange. The building had recently been refurbished so it looked good but was underused. Its purpose wasn't clear and it had never really found its feet, despite being open for a couple of years. We had a very clear vision for the Grange: we wanted a multi-use centre, well used by the community and financially self-sustaining, and we achieved that within twelve months."

Claire Evans, 4CT Chief Executive (former JOG Co-ordinator).

20 05

1st February

Tony Blair is back in east Manchester, this time meeting residents for an early morning cuppa in the Grange from where he is interviewed by GMTV.

24th February

East magazine is launched.

Produced by regeneration photographer and writer Len Grant, the first issue follows the construction of *B of the Bang* and examines the economic benefits enjoyed by local pubs after Manchester City's move to east Manchester. (A further nine issues are published until 2009 when *East* goes online at www.thisiseast.com).

east

The Sky Blue Pound
B of the Bang...
rising star?
Elizabeth Wells at 103
Carnival King

March

Youth Strategy launched.

With lots of organisations responsible for providing services to young people it seems like a good idea to pull it all together. New Deal and New East Manchester work with their partners, Manchester Youth Service, the voluntary sector, Sports Development and Leisure Services, to make sure all the agencies are co-ordinating their support for the benefit of east Manchester's young people.

"In my view, the greatest thing to come out of New Deal has been the multi-agency working. It's so easy now for people to get around a table and solve problems together. That still doesn't happen elsewhere but it's crucial and works on so many different levels."

Jeff Burns, Community Development Manager.

There have been 114 fewer burglaries and 82 fewer vehicle crimes in 2005 than in 2000.
Source: NDC administrative data from Social Disadvantage Research Centre, University of Oxford.

July

Philips Park is awarded Green Flag status (and gets it every year since).

The Green Flag award scheme was set up by the Civic Trust in 1996 as a way of recognising and rewarding the best green spaces in the country. It sets a benchmark of excellence in recreational green areas and encourages others to follow.

31st March

4CT established by the merger of Joint Openshaw Group (JOG), Clayton Community Association and Bradford and Beswick Community Group.

"I was representing JOG (Joint Openshaw Group) on the board of the Bradford and Beswick Community Group at the time and we were discussing whether we could take on the administration of a small grants fund. Some board members thought it was risky, a bit too much responsibility. As we considered the different skills we could pool between the two groups, Barbara [Taylor] just said, out of exasperation almost, 'Why don't we just merge!' and so, 18 months and a lot of hard work later, we did.

"It seemed inappropriate to have Bradford and Beswick merge with Openshaw but not include Clayton, so we invited Clayton Community Association to come on board too.

"It was originally going to be called 3CT – three communities together – but that name had already been taken, so we decided on 4CT – Beswick, Clayton, Openshaw and Bradford – short and snappy. It doesn't really matter if people don't know what it stands for."

Claire Evans, 4CT Chief Executive (former JOG Co-ordinator).

May

Clayton Children's Centre opens next to the Wells Centre.

Things can only get better. 69% of residents are 'satisfied' with their neighbourhood in 2005. The figure was 59% in 2002 and only 46% in 1999.
Source: NEM Household Perception Survey 1999, 2002, 2005.

Transport for all   The 'Beacons Brother' tent

May
Launch of East Manchester Community Transport.

July

"During the summer of 2005 – at the height of Channel 4's *Big Brother* success – we set up a 'Beacons Brother' tent at the Parties in the Park. It was one of our Pride in East Manchester initiatives, (see opposite).

"There was a guy hidden and when you walked into the tent you could hear his voice, but you couldn't see him. And it was done up just like the Big Brother diary room! He'd be asking probing questions and gently get people's views of the improvements in the area. We filmed it all and then edited it into a video. It was a fun way of eliciting opinions from people who wouldn't fill in a questionnaire or come to a meeting but still had something to say about their area."

Lesley Spencer, Senior Regeneration Officer.

25th July
New Sportcity Visitor Centre opens.

On the third anniversary of the Games, the Sportcity Visitor Centre is officially opened by Clayton resident and Games volunteer Mandy Gilchrest, with cycling supremo Victoria Pendleton and Kit, the Games mascot.

24th August
Cabinet Office Minister Jim Murphy MP visits Eastserve to mark the launch of Phase 3 of the largest IT project of its kind in Europe. As well as the 3,500 Beacons residents who have enjoyed the subsidised broadband and hardware offers, a further 1,700 residents in Miles Platting, Ancoats, Newton Heath and Gorton will also benefit.

Pride in East Manchester.

"We needed a way of making sure the hardest to reach residents were getting involved in the Beacons programme. So 'Pride' was a two-year project to engage those who wouldn't normally engage.

"We'd go out to different events – Chinese New Year, Refugee Week, Parties in the Park and use unusual techniques to encourage people to open up.

"In 2005 there was the 'Beacons Brother' diary room (see opposite) and at another time there was a photography project where residents were invited to write on special whiteboards which had statements like: 'I'm proud of east Manchester because...' and 'For east Manchester I want...' These worked very well and we got lots of interesting comments. 'Tops and Pants' was a fun follow-up to that which toured the 2006 Parties in the Park (see page 148).

"You couldn't use any of the information we gathered in any meaningful, statistical way – it was only ever a general perception – but it worked because we did talk to people we wouldn't normally have spoken to and we did get some important feedback. As an example, people were saying there weren't enough activities for young people when actually there was *loads* to do. Clearly it was a communication problem so we re-assessed our publicity: where we put it, what languages it was in, and how we distributed it, so more young people could get involved.

"The wristbands were all the rage at the time, so we produced our own orange and blue ones as part of the Pride programme. Everyone was wearing them, including government ministers!"

Lesley Spencer, Senior Regeneration Officer.

FOR EAST MANCHESTER I WANT

more trips out in School

FOR EAST MANCHESTER I WANT

MORE CONCERTS AT THE STADIUM

I'M PROUD OF EAST MANCHESTER BECAUSE

I like playing tennis at the tennis centre.

FOR EAST MANCHESTER I WANT

MORE PARKS

I'M PROUD OF EAST MANCHESTER BECAUSE

We love drumming!

FOR EAST MANCHESTER I WANT

I like proximity to the City centre.

Other facilities, sports, schools, stadium

I'M PROUD OF EAST MANCHESTER BECAUSE

OF THE GRANGE

August

Over 600 young people from regeneration areas across the region – including 50 or so from east Manchester – take part in the first North West Street Games. Minister for Sport, Richard Caborn MP, comes along to check it out. (The Beacons own Street Games in the following February half-term prove to be as popular, with activities like rock climbing, martial arts, badminton, graffiti art and breakdancing.)

20
05

> "We had meetings with all the North West regeneration initiatives where we'd network and share best practice. At one of those meetings we decided to stage a big sports event in the summer holidays at a 'multi-facility venue' – only Sportcity fitted the bill – and invite kids from all these different areas. On the day we mixed everyone up so there might have been someone from Liverpool in the same team as someone from east Manchester and Salford. (The year after we changed that around because the kids said they'd prefer to be with their mates.) It was a great day with a fantastic atmosphere."
>
> **John Dwan, former Sport Action Zone Manager.**

3rd October

Wristband for Miliband.

David Miliband MP, Minister for Communities and Local Government, meets resident board representatives at the Grange including Irene Baron, Elaine Wright, Linda Wagner and Jeff Burns, who present him with a Pride in East Manchester wristband.

8th October 2005

"Don't you scrub up well?!"

Five-year celebration event at the City of Manchester Stadium.

"It was a really good mix of staff, partners, residents and volunteers, about 300 altogether. It felt like the right thing at the right time... and it was absolutely fabulous!"

Sean McGonigle.

"It was wonderful, seeing everyone dressed up to the nines. Everyone had made an effort and it was beautiful to see. There were lots of residents and agencies but it wasn't about who did what, it was just about celebrating how far we'd come in those first five years. I'll always remember that."

Andrea Melarkey, Clayton resident.

"I objected to them spending that kind of money on a five-year party. I was going to get a star, but I told them they could stick it, I didn't want a star. I didn't go. I can justify a celebration at the end of ten years, but not after five, it was a waste of money and I told them straight."

Barbara Taylor, Beswick resident.

"People were arriving in limousines. You couldn't even imagine limousines in east Manchester ten years ago. It wouldn't have happened. They'd have said it wasn't worth the insurance risk.

"At one point there were loads of people on the stage getting awards and everyone in the room just stood and clapped and clapped. It was lovely. And every song they played seemed to mean something to each community group. Ours was *Things Can Only Get Better*. We used to play it a lot in the early days, more out of defiance really, you know, because *surely* things couldn't get any worse... they could only get better... and they *did* get better."

Wendy Eaton, Openshaw resident.

"I can honestly say, I didn't have the faintest idea I was getting the Anne Brady Good Neighbour Award. When I went up on stage, and I could see everyone standing up applauding, I was so proud. For once in my life, I was totally gobsmacked, I didn't know what to say. I've never done anything for a reward, if you understand me, it's not my way, but I am proud of that and the trophy is still on the side there."

Bill Booth, first winner of the Anne Brady Memorial Award for being a Good Neighbour.

"Although she was officially our cleaner, Anne would spot you through the window in the morning and, by the time you'd parked your car, walked in and got to your desk, she'd have a cuppa and a piece of toast there waiting for you... just for the ones who came in early. She was like your mother really. We really miss her."

Lesley Spencer, Principal Regeneration Officer.

Bill Booth receives his award from Liam Brady, Anne's husband.

3rd November

Tony Blair visits east Manchester and meets a number of residents – including Andrea Melarkey, Diane Vickers and Janet McGlashen – at the Wells Centre in Clayton to talk about crime and antisocial behaviour.

"We only found out who it was when we got there. When I walked into the room there were names on the seats. My name was on one seat, then a blank one, and then Wendy's. So I'm thinking, I wonder who's going to be sat there, between us? But he was lovely, really pleasant. He asked us how our crime initiatives had improved the area, and he was genuinely interested in what we had to say. We've come on leaps and bounds, so it was a really positive meeting. But I was amazed at how thin his knees were! That's all I could think about after: weren't his knees thin!"

Andrea Melarkey, Clayton resident.

25th November

The Intensive Support project scoops a prestigious employment award at the Office of the Deputy Prime Minister's New Deal for Communities and Neighbourhood Management Awards. The project, which has been running for three years, supports long-term unemployed residents with mental health issues, drug and alcohol problems, people with criminal records, the homeless, single-parent families, people with disabilities and refugees and asylum seekers.

November

East Manchester is selected to run a Youth Advisors pilot for the Neighbourhood Renewal Unit. The idea is to encourage the participation of young people in the regeneration of their communities. The scheme identifies young people who represent their peers and who can tell 'the powers that be' what's needed. They advise community leaders and decision-makers how they can be more engaged in community life. Of the six east Manchester advisors, three cover the Beacons area: Danny Robinson representing Beswick; Leonie Gasper, Openshaw; and Emma Richardson, Clayton. (Nationally there are now 450 young advisors!)

Thank you

For putting your heart into the regeneration of **East Manchester**

NEW DEAL for EAST MANCHESTER

"We were about half way through our programme and we just wanted to say 'Thanks!' to everyone for sticking with it."

Sean McGonigle.

This is National Reading Champion Paul Sleem promoting his Mission Possible reading scheme at Ashbury Meadow Primary School.

Since becoming the Education Action Zone's Literacy Champion, Paul has recruited 120 local volunteers to the 'Read Together' project in primary schools and introduced other initiatives to show pupils and their families that reading can be fun.

November

Greater Manchester Police's Safer Neighbourhoods Team is launched across Beswick and Openshaw to provide a more visible and responsive service for the local community. The team of Police Constables and Police Community Support Officers will attend resident group meetings, visit sheltered accommodation, youth clubs, and local colleges. They will increase their patrols in areas considered 'hot spots' by local residents, remove untaxed vehicles and generally work even more closely with the community to make east Manchester safer.

January

The Regeneration Assistants project is awarded 'exemplar status' from the RENEW Centre of Excellence. RENEW Northwest is the organisation set up by the Northwest Regional Development Agency in 2005 to promote regeneration best practice. Three of the assistants and Gary Lamb, the Project Co-ordinator, are nominated for awards.

The first cohort of assistants also become the first students in the country to achieve Level 2 of the Working in the Community qualification. One has now moved onto the Level 3 qualification and the others are the first to undertake a newly developed foundation degree in Neighbourhood Renewal at Salford University.

25th January

Manchester City FC donates oak trees to east Manchester parks.

In recognition of receiving a Gold Environmental Business Pledge Award, Manchester City Football Club donates 11 oak trees, representing the 11 players, which are then planted in east Manchester parks.

30th January

The Intelligent Community Forum, an international not-for-profit think tank, includes east Manchester in its annual list of Top Seven Intelligent Communities of the world. It's thanks to Eastserve that east Manchester makes the list as competing communities are judged against five key indicators that define the competitive edge in a broadband economy.

February

Equality Works: it's in the name.

"This was all about carrying forward the incredible work we were doing around social inclusion. We had already launched the Toolkit the year before (see page 122) so Equality Works was moving things up a gear.

"It was essentially a marketing event for public services to encourage them to embed equality in the very core of what they did. We wanted to change the culture in organisations – including our own – where equality became everyone's responsibility. We were saying, 'It's not complicated, it's not time-consuming, it's not expensive... it's just a fine tuning.'

"We organised training, got commitment and then had a follow-up event 12 months later to celebrate success."

Philip Bradley, Principal Regeneration Officer.

February

The Money Mentors team stage a 'Chic on the Cheap' fashion show at Sportcity where residents receive tips on looking good on a budget.

Brought up on what he describes as an 'extremely challenging council estate', Nick Buckley was not, at first, keen to get a regular job. After turning down a place at university, working as a cocktail barman, market trader, aircraft dispatcher, and travelling the world in between, he had little idea his next move would lead to a career steering young people away from crime.

I came back broke from a two-year world trip and decided I needed to find a new job, something satisfying and enjoyable. One morning I picked up a pile of junk mail from the mat and was just about to bin it all when I saw a leaflet promoting careers in regeneration. I applied for the Regeneration Assistant position, was interviewed, and got one of the first four places on the new programme.

For the first year we were given experience in all the different departments of NDC and New East Manchester. Every six weeks you'd turn up at a new desk with new people and learn how they contributed to the regeneration effort.

While I was working in the crime and disorder team a half-time post came up as a Youth Intervention Officer. That was the area I was really keen on developing so I pooled my Regeneration Assistant time and became a Youth Intervention Officer full-time.

With the police we'd target those young people whose offences maybe weren't that serious but, if left unchecked, could lead to a criminal career. We'd bring them and their parents down to the station, read them the riot act, point out the choices they faced and, if they were receptive, I'd work with them to access training and educational opportunities.

Having come from the same background I know myself how easy it is to get in trouble with the police. Boredom plays a big part. It's even harder these days with gangs and guns and drugs. Bad parenting leads to more bad parenting: some mums and dads just don't know any different. I know the only reason I didn't get into trouble myself was because I had the support of a loving and secure family.

From Youth Intervention Officer I moved on to become a Community Safety Co-ordinator in north Manchester and am now working in that same role with Greater Manchester Police in the city centre.

It's been an incredibly rewarding journey so far and, as I still live in the area, I frequently meet young people whom I've been able to help and they tell me how they've changed direction after our intervention and how they're at college or wherever. Of course, there are some who you didn't get through to, but you can't win them all.

Nick Buckley with PC Andy Costello

6th March

Treasury Minister Des Browne MP meets residents at the Grange in Beswick where he stumbles across a belly-dancing class.

March

Come on Down!... Advice is Your Right!

Loosely based on the game show *The Price is Right*, young people at Crossley House in Openshaw learn what their local councillors get up to and how to contact them as well as how to get help and advice on schools, housing, jobs and health.

10th March

The Medlock Valley gets £2 million.

The public open space alongside the River Medlock is to receive nearly £2 million of funding. £1.7 million of this will come from the Northwest Regional Development Agency for a three-year programme of work that will enhance the whole Medlock Valley including Clayton Vale and Philips Park, one of the first municipal parks.

In the last five years there has been a 27% increase in the proportion of pupils aged 17 and 18 staying on in full-time education. By 2006 45% now stay on after 16.
Source: NDC administrative data from Social Disadvantage Research Centre, University of Oxford.

March

The booklet *Beacons for Change: Pride, Passion and Pergolas* is launched to celebrate the completion of the Community Environment Programme.

"In the early days people were knocking on our door demanding change to their local environment. It was such a big issue, everyone was affected. The success of the Community Environment Programme has underpinned the regeneration of the whole area and this book was our way of capturing the essence of that programme and the efforts of the people involved. It's one small book that speaks volumes."

Julie Lawrence, Environmental Programme Manager.

Community Spirit is Back!

It was one of New Deal's first projects to get off the ground, an opportunity for what NDC's Co-ordinator Sean McGonigle calls an 'early win'. Working closely with residents and their environment partner, Groundwork, NDC embarked on a sustained and hugely successful programme of reclaiming the local area.

New parks and play areas were created, existing ones vastly improved. Dull terraced streets sprang into life with colourful planters and hanging baskets; derelict land became communal gardens; sculptures were commissioned. Even disused buildings were demolished and replaced with garden extensions.

Most significantly, the Community Environment Programme, introduced 'alleygating' where back alleys of terraced houses, typically used as dumping grounds and easy access for opportunistic burglars, were gated and enclosed. With small grants residents quickly transformed their back alleys and small disused crofts into beautiful gardens where neighbours socialised and a community spirit returned.

"We got what we wanted through New Deal giving us the power to say what we wanted rather than being told what we're having."

Andrea Melarkey, Clayton resident.

"You look at what they've done with the alleygating scheme and it's brilliant. It's not just about putting a gate at the back of some properties, it's what they've done behind that gate. Derelict land is transformed into places where people can sit out, meet up, and communicate. You've got the older people – who no-one would normally see – getting out there and chatting to the younger ones. Now everyone knows their neighbours, there's a real bond within the community.

"At first I was sceptical about Groundwork but, after working closely with them, they have to be one of the best, if not the best, environmental agency to work with."

Steve Green, Openshaw resident.

"NDC gave us the opportunity to be creative and innovative. There weren't any off-the-shelf solutions to the problems in east Manchester but we were given the flexibility to try new things. Coming up with fresh ideas is part of what we do and, with careful research and consultation with all the partners, we hit on some sustainable solutions. The alleygating doesn't seem particularly innovative now, but it – and many other new approaches – was rolled out over the city, and many other cities.

"As well as new gardens, cleaned-up spaces and safe, communal back alleys, the programme gave people confidence in what could be achieved. These things had never really happened before."

Jason Brindle, Groundwork MSSTT.

"We bid for a Green Streets award and won an environmental makeover worth £120,000. Groundwork managed the finances but residents developed the ideas. The tots and teenagers worked with the older residents and came up with the enchanted forest theme. It was like a TV garden makeover programme but on a larger scale!"

Irene Johnson, Beswick resident.

March

The East Manchester Play Forum is set up.

"Every summer, JOG [Joint Openshaw Group, a small voluntary group] would organise activities for children in local parks. With a variety of partners they'd help keep young people entertained and occupied. It worked really well and we put some money in.

"When the Play Forum was set up the summer play scheme was one of the projects we highlighted as good practice and it was rolled out across Manchester. The citywide, year-round 'Parktastic' scheme is a direct result of those play schemes."

Philip Bradley, Principal Regeneration Officer.

5th May

Ward co-ordination meeting with a difference.

"This was led by the Young Advisors and they really put some of the service providers on the spot. They raised concerns about all sorts of things including their own personal safety and about highways issues. Parks, they felt, were dominated by older young people often involved in criminal behaviour, and the police were challenged to be more supportive. It was actually a very constructive meeting, and another best practice example."

Lesley Spencer, Senior Regeneration Officer.

June

Thos. Storey Fabrications Ltd transfer their Stockport operation to a new factory in Openshaw.

Thos. Storey were the original manufacturers of the Second World War 'Bailey Bridge' system. Now they make digger buckets, fuel and hydraulic tanks, chassis etc.

"We not only helped Thos. Storey find the right premises for their expansion but also built a solid working relationship with them.

"At the time of Thos. Storey's move to Openshaw, MANCAT (later The Manchester College) were considering withdrawing their welding course because they no longer saw a demand for it, although our Business Advisors were advising me to the contrary. We brought half a dozen metal fabricators together, including Thos. Storey, to examine how they each worked. They concluded they each had different peaks and troughs in their demand for skilled welders, and so we developed a labour-sharing programme with them – not unlike the beginnings of Aspire (see page 102) – where they could share the workforce between them. This convinced the college to stick with the course and we ran a massive recruitment drive for trainee welders."

Carol Bartram, Head of Economic Development.

7th July

The trams will finally roll into east Manchester.

Douglas Alexander announces partnership funding for Phase 3 of Metrolink. Tracks will be laid as far as Droylsden towards Ashton and to the new station at Central Park as part of the Oldham and Rochdale extension.

July

Parties in the Park.

More fun in the sun with the annual parties in east Manchester parks. This year, as part of the Pride in East Manchester programme (see page 131), there is a 'Tops and Pants' consultation where everyone gets to write what they think is tops or pants about the area on pieces of card clothing and pin them on a washing line!

August

Mini Movie Makers: not for grown-ups.

"This was about acknowledging that young people also had opinions that mattered. We wanted them to stay in east Manchester, work here, and bring their own kids up here, so their opinions on how the community should develop were equally valid. We brought a group together who made a video in the style of a news report – it was called *Mission Possible* – and then distributed the DVD across the area."

Tracey Annette, former Resident Liaison Officer.

26th September

Sporting Edge kicks off.

The sports hall of the former St Peter's School in Higher Openshaw is to be converted into a sports facility for local people. Manchester City FC's manager Stuart Pearce and a couple of his star players – Paul Dickov and Darius Vassell – mark the start on site with local schoolchildren.

26th November

The Best Bar None Off Licence Awards are held at Manchester's Hilton Hotel. Ten local off licences receive accreditations for their part in discouraging alcohol misuse.

4th December

The Neighbour Nuisance Team and the Warden Service formally merge to form the Eastlands Homes Community Safety Team. The wardens change their uniforms from blue to red to embrace Eastlands Homes corporate colours. They continue to patrol Beswick, Clayton and Openshaw and now patrol Gorton North, South and West. The service remains available to all residents whether tenant or homeowner.

"The wardens have been special, very special. You knew most of them because they lived in the same area. I'd always call them before the police, not that the police don't do a brilliant job, it was just that I knew the wardens would deal with it more... personally really.

"I know things change and that funding changes but I'm disappointed the warden service isn't the same as it was when we first set it up. I relied on the wardens a lot, and now I don't really have any contact with them. I'm finding that hard to get my head round."

Andrea Melarkey, Clayton resident.

December

People like us.

"In the December we organised a trip to see *Mamma Mia* at the Palace. Ring and Ride had brought everyone to the Grange where we had fish and chips from Tony's before we left. While we were having our supper, one lady in her seventies, said to me, 'I'm really looking froward to this. I'm really excited.' Well we all were, it had a really good reputation. But then she said, 'I've never been to a show before. It's not really for people like us, is it?' When we came out after the show, this lady got hold of my hand really tight. Her eyes were sparkling, like a little kid in the sweet shop. 'Oh!' she said, 'I've really enjoyed it. Thanks for giving me the opportunity to go.' And then, as we walked to the coach she said, 'People told me I shouldn't come into town. They said there'd be fights and guns. But it's not bad here is it?' That makes it all worthwhile for me, giving people new experiences even at that age. That's what regeneration is all about."

Dot Rathbone, DARTS [Days Away for Recycled Teenagers] organiser.

30th January 2007

The 'super casino' is awarded to east Manchester.

In 2005 The Gambling Act allowed the creation of one regional or 'super casino' and a number of smaller ones. To assess the applicants an independent Casino Advisory Panel, chaired by Professor Stephen Crow, was set up by the Department for Culture, Media and Sport. On the decision day in January 2007, journalists were waiting in Blackpool and at the O2 (formerly the Millennium Dome) in Greenwich, as these were considered the hot favourites.

The announcement that east Manchester had won came as a surprise to everyone, not least the City Council who hurriedly arranged a press conference at the City of Manchester Stadium as the press raced down from Blackpool.

Within a couple of months of the original decision, east Manchester's super casino was under threat. Many MPs would have preferred the casino to be awarded to Blackpool. The Casino Advisory Panel's decision was narrowly supported in the Commons by just 24 votes, but defeated in the House of Lords by three votes. Confusion continued until Gordon Brown, in only his second prime minister's questions, announced: "I hope that during the summer months we can look at regeneration in areas earmarked for the super casino. There may be a better way of meeting the economic and social needs than the creation of super casinos."

Angry City Council officers and Manchester MPs lobbied the Government for an alternative to the super casino, and eventually, in 2010, an announcement was made about the future of the site.

"Locally we pushed the idea that it would bring massive benefits to the area and many people got behind us. But there were plenty of residents who didn't get what it was all about and were only influenced by what they saw or read. They saw it only as a casino and not as a boost to the local economy. But there wasn't a great groundswell of opinion one way or the other, people were fairly neutral in their reaction to getting it ... and then to losing it."

Sean McGonigle.

"While some people are understandably disappointed that the jobs the casino could have brought will not now come to east Manchester, many local people are delighted that the voice of the communities most affected by all this at last have a chance to speak about alternative options that we think offer much more promise than the idea of a casino. We are delighted that Gordon Brown and government ministers are listening to what people really want."

Local resident Sandra Webb on behalf of Communities for Stability.

When **Denise Marchant** moved to Clayton from the other side of the city it was because she was worried about drugs. She was looking for her first house to buy and, in the early 80s, east Manchester was the only place affordable. Unwelcome at first, she and her family gradually became accepted in what was a traditional working-class community. Since her children have grown up, she's become a neighbourhood warden, serving the area she now calls home.

I was very happy living in Hulme. The sense of community was great but then the drugs came and they were dealing right there on the street. I didn't want my children brought up around that and, because I wasn't a priority for the council, I didn't qualify for an exchange. So I decided to buy my own place and Clayton fell within my price range, which wasn't much.

My children are mixed race and, as there were no other black children in our new neighbourhood in those days, it felt like we'd swapped the potential drug and gang problems for a whole load of racial issues.

Ever since New Deal set up the warden service and I saw them patrolling the streets, I've always wanted to do this job. I've worked for the council for many years and I've also taken time out to do voluntary work. It was while I was working with the Clayton Community Centre that I met Ray, one of the first wardens. I'd often ask him if there were any vacancies – it became a bit of a joke after a while – and then one day he said, yes, there were some new posts available and encouraged me to apply. So I did and I got the job! And I have to say I love being a neighbourhood warden, I absolutely love it.

They call us the eyes and ears of the community and that's a key part of our role. We support victims of crime and help them with home security. We also work closely with neighbour nuisance officers, reporting anti-social behaviour, and with street environment officers to tackle graffiti and rubbish. People also report crime to us; some find it easier to approach us than the police.

I remember one night there was a large group of youths on one of the local parks and, although the police were there, we knew an elderly resident who lived facing the park would be distressed. When we arrived he was watching all the commotion from his bedroom window. We parked our vehicle in front of his house, called him up and reassured him that we wouldn't move until everyone had dispersed. And that's exactly what we did. It's great to know you've helped someone feel safe in their own home.

March

Police Inspector Steve McFarlane, Community Safety Co-ordinator Paul Cullen and Safer Neighbourhood Co-ordinator Karen Hopes win the GMP Chief Constable's Excellence Award in the partnership working category.

The team devised Operation Axel in east Manchester, a joint agency approach to patrolling, intelligence gathering, civil and criminal enforcement, with activities to divert teenagers away from crime and targeting under-age drinking. Axel achieved a 25% overall reduction in youth nuisance calls.

March

A Guide to a Healthier Me booklet is delivered door-to-door with information and tips on how to lead a more active and healthy lifestyle.

March

"Our first annual report was a very dry document which no-one read. Since then we've tried to make each report more informal, more fun. One year the theme was 'Have a Read, Have a Brew', with a tea bag inside a small booklet. We continued the theme the following year when we delivered a free tea towel door-to-door, printed with all the project details. Another was a colouring book with pictures designed by local resident Bob Wright – I'm sure I recognised some of the cartoon characters he created! Government Office were initially taken aback with tea towels as annual reports but we were later applauded for best practice in our engagement techniques."

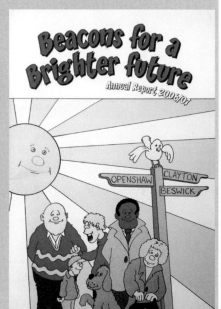

Lesley Spencer,
Senior Regeneration Officer.

In 1999 only 9.1% of under 21s were accepted into higher education. Now it's 15.5%, a 70% increase.
Source: NDC administrative data from Social Disadvantage Research Centre, University of Oxford.

May

Sporting Edge is ready!

Created from the refurbishment of the former St. Peter's School sports hall, the new £1.1 million centre opens its doors to the local community. There's football, cricket, basketball, rugby, and badminton as well as a community space and computer suite with training and free internet access.

June

Openshaw's new health centre opens.

As well as the GPs' surgery there are ante-natal, midwifery and physiotherapy services.

"Our current building has served Higher Openshaw for over half a century but it is now too small and old-fashioned. The new purpose-built centre will provide our existing patients with first class medical care and allow us to re-open our list so we can take on new people from the rapidly growing local population. The size and design of the building will allow for the ever changing requirements of our community."

Dr Gary O'Driscoll (whose family has run a GP practice in Openshaw for over 70 years).

"Standing, for the first time, in front of the completed health centre has got to count amongst my highlights. The O'Driscolls had been due to move into a healthy living centre we'd planned, but that didn't happen, so we had to find somewhere very quickly for them – a new building – and we pulled that off, so that was very important."

Libby Graham, Director of Social Programmes.

2007

12th June

Michael Kenyon wins the Anne Brady Memorial Award for being a Good Neighbour.

Stella Quainoo from Groundwork says, "Michael Kenyon is an example to us all. He is constantly helping others around him yet never accepts any thanks for all his hard work. Although all the neighbours appreciate what he does, official recognition as east Manchester's Good Neighbour 2007 is the pat on the back he really deserves."

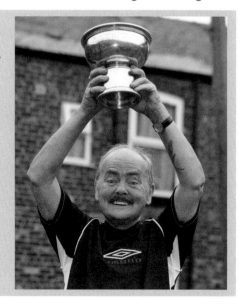

27th June

All change at the top: Gordon Brown comes to power. Ten days later...

6th July

Sven-Göran Eriksson is confirmed as the new manager of Manchester City FC.

19th September

Top awards for east Manchester!

New East Manchester is named Regeneration Agency of the Year and the pioneering Regeneration Assistants Training Scheme scoops the top award in the training category at the first Regeneration and Renewal Magazine Awards. One of the judges said: "One of the things we liked about New East Manchester is that it combines physical investment and physical change with community involvement and developing the social capital base of residents."

NEM Chief Executive Tom Russell collects the Agency of the Year Award

September

The Super Respect Youth Nuisance scheme kicks off and runs for six months. Lots of agencies get involved to provide – amongst other things – diversionary activities on Friday and Saturday evenings for the young people of Clayton. The project is highly commended in the social regeneration-led category at the 2008 Regeneration and Renewal Magazine Awards.

20
07

October

Life after New Deal.

New Deal for Communities merges with New East Manchester to ensure a consistent approach to regeneration across the whole area and guarantee that the legacy of the Beacons programme lives on after March 2010 when the NDC funding ends.

> "We have learnt from other time-restrictive programmes (like Hulme City Challenge and different rounds of the Single Regeneration Budget), that planning for the exit needs to be done, at a minimum, two years before the closure date. It has given time for New Deal's wider stakeholder group to adjust and for New East Manchester to underpin the structures and governance arrangements that were in place."
>
> **Eddie Smith, Chief Executive, New East Manchester.**

November

The new EnterPrize award aims to encourage local businesses and entrepreneurs in east Manchester. At the finals, business mentor and broadcaster Rachel Elnaugh (*Dragons' Den* and *Red Letter Days*) presents the awards and spends the evening talking to guests and budding entrepreneurs. And the winner is... computer software design company Smart Plan.

18th October

Openshaw resident Elaine Wright receives her MBE at Buckingham Palace for Services to the Community of east Manchester.

Elaine with proud son Darren and husband Bob

October

Let's Talk.

Dozens of consultation events are held in October and November to hear residents' opinions on New East Manchester's Strategic Regeneration Framework, the plan for the next ten years.

> "There was never going to be any substantial change to what was originally planned for east Manchester. Our analysis had always been that only large-scale transformational change was going to make a significant difference to people's lives here. We were basically asking whether people were up for it. But there was fine detail we would have missed if we hadn't talked to local people about their experiences. At the end of the process, I remember going through 70 or 80 comments and observations that needed to be reflected in our final document."
>
> **Tom Russell, former Chief Executive, New East Manchester.**

2nd November

The community radio station, ALL FM East Manchester, throw a launch party attended by the Lord Mayor of Manchester and local celebrity model Lisa Sabel.

> "We used to fund a temporary radio station – East Manchester FM – developed by Radio Regen and running for a week at a time. I remember being 'ambushed' on it for about two hours one evening after they'd invited about three or four residents into the studio to give me a hard time.
>
> "Now we support ALL FM East Manchester, who've been extremely successful in other parts of the city and now broadcast from here every week. I drop in regularly and answer listeners' questions. Now the radio station is as much part of our social programme as it is part of our communications strategy."
>
> **Sean McGonigle.**

20 08

November

Eastlands Homes is awarded more than £160,000 by the Big Lottery Fund to set up a project that will support children showing early signs of disruptive behaviour.

The Early Intervention Support Project will work closely with six- to twelve-year-olds in east Manchester whose behaviour is at risk of getting worse.

March

Smart Plan, the computer software design company that won the first EnterPrize last year, launches an online tool that will revolutionise the UK planning application process. Founder Maciej Orzechowski, 37, has used his award of £10,000 to develop

the prototype for Smart Designer, a computerised personal architect and automated planning application tool. He has raised further investment, taken on a business partner and is in talks with a number of major DIY chains interested in retailing his new product.

What do residents think now? In 1999, 28% thought the quality of their home was 'good' or 'very good'. Now it's 63%. In 1999, only 2% thought sports and leisure provision was 'good' or 'very good'. Now it's 53%. And 60% think the same about their parks compared to only 12% back in 1999.

Source: NEM Household Perception Survey 1999 and 2008.

14th May 2008

The 2008 UEFA Cup final is staged at City of Manchester Stadium.

Zenit St Petersburg 2, Rangers 0.

The generally good-natured event is marred by violence in Manchester city centre as frustrated Rangers fans clash with police after an outdoor screen failed during the match.

13th July

The urban obstacle course...

The first Urbanathlon is run in east Manchester.

Over 600 competitors clamber over rock climbing walls, stagger up terracing at the stadium, vault over derelict cars... all for fun.

On the same sunny day...

Rather than taking place in four local parks, this summer's Party in the Park is centred on Philips Park and features the first Seeds of the East festival. There are performance artists, workshops, a Royal Horticultural Society Q&A, and schoolchildren's shows. The adjacent community orchard and allotments all get stuck in, entertaining and educating the party-goers.

July

Signage duo win £10,000 EnterPrize award.

Peter Potts and Westley McKay lost their jobs 18 months ago when the signmaking firm they worked for went into receivership. Determined not to let their combined expertise go to waste, the two friends bought equipment from the liquidator and set up Built-Up Signs. The rest, as they say...

September 2008

Eastlands Homes celebrates its fifth birthday.

Since 2003 around £16,000 has been spent on each of 2,800 properties across east Manchester as part of a £45 million improvement programme.

More than 14,000 improvements have been carried out, including:

- **2,637 double glazed windows and doors**
- **2,453 new kitchens**
- **2,456 roofs and insulation improvements**
- **2,030 electrical rewiring jobs**

"In the old days you'd phone up for a repair, right? It could be the most minor thing in the world, but by time they got round to doing it, it'd be a major one. I've known tenants who could put their fingers through the bloody window frames. Eastlands Homes has made a helluva difference since then."

Maggie Warburton, Clayton resident.

1st October

JobCity at Sportcity.

900 job-seekers talk to potential employers and get support and advice at JobCity at the City of Manchester Stadium.

October

Eastlands Homes becomes the 'registered social landlord' for around 5,400 council-owned homes in Gorton, Longsight, Levenshulme, Ardwick and Rusholme.

18th November

Thomas Heatherwick Studio Ltd, the design team behind the beleaguered *B of the Bang* sculpture, agrees to pay the City Council £1.7 million in an out-of-court settlement after structural problems remain unresolved.

December

Dog services scoop awards.

Two entrepreneurs running successful dog services firms win the first and second prizes at the EnterPrize awards ceremony.

Barking Barbers, a holistic dog grooming company based in Beswick, wins the top prize of £10,000. Hound Helpers, a dog-walking and pet-sitting business in Gorton, wins the £5,000 runner-up award.

15th March 2009

Fun Run in Clayton Vale.

Diane Modahl, former Commonwealth champion and Olympian, sets 90 mums, dads and kids off on a 2km race around the Vale. Her 13-year-old daughter, Imani, is first across the finish line.

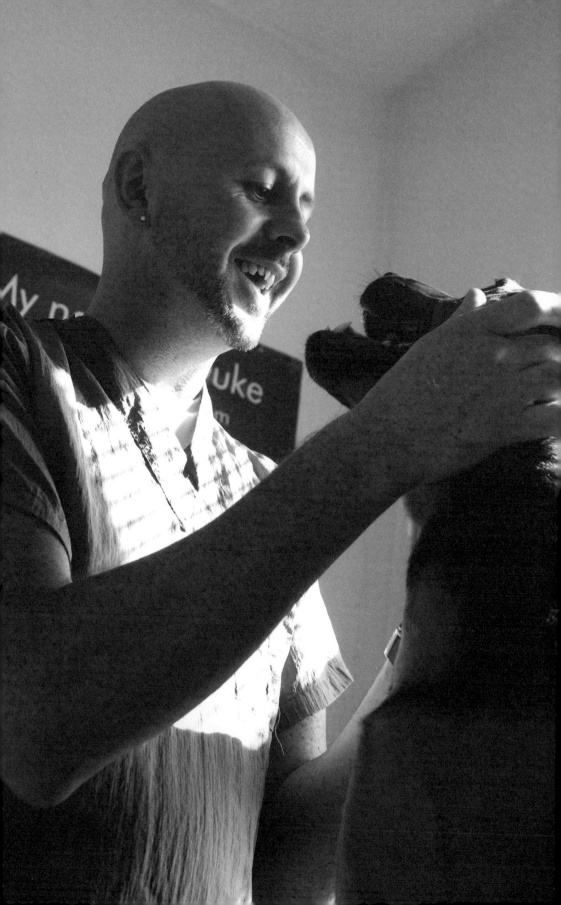

Angel Moore loves dogs. His clients know this and, more importantly, their dogs know it too. Setting up in business as a holistic dog groomer has not been easy but New East Manchester has been supportive from the first tentative steps back in 2006. Then, in December 2008, Barking Barbers won the £10,000 first prize in the EnterPrize business competition and Angel has big plans for the future.

I was working as a florist when I first came to Manchester in 2002. The Games were on and the place was really buzzing, but I wasn't enjoying work. I felt I was in the rat race and desperately needed a change.

One of my friends, who knew I was crazy about dogs, suggested I try dog grooming and so I did, and took to it like a duck to water. I completed a one-year course and learnt all the conventional techniques but I knew from the start I didn't want to be an ordinary groomer. My life priorities were changing and, to tie in with my Buddhist beliefs, I wanted to find an ethical way of making a living, so I became a holistic groomer which means I treat each dog individually according to their needs. I guess I am unique in that respect and yes, my clients do say I have an affinity with their pets. It certainly makes the job rewarding when a client arrives and their dog is excited to see me.

After my course one of the business advisors from New East Manchester worked closely with me to develop a business plan and help me apply for a grant which paid for the computers and hardware I needed to get started. They kept offering me courses to attend – web design, e-commerce, marketing – and I snapped them all up, which has made a massive difference and saved me a huge amount of money. There can't be many dog groomers who understand search engine optimisation! The website has made more people aware of what we have to offer and we're now receiving orders from as far away as Japan.

Winning the EnterPrize award has been fantastic. The advice from the judges through each of the preliminary rounds was invaluable in its own right, and, well, when they announced Barking Barbers as the winners, I was over the moon. I honestly didn't think I stood a chance as the competition was intense: there are some great small businesses in east Manchester.

In October 2009 I opened my flagship store in east Manchester and now employ four members of staff.

2009

16th March

Beverley Hughes MP undertakes the handover of Eastserve to Symera, a private company awarded a concession agreement to manage and invest in the local internet project.

27th March

Ground-breaking on the East Manchester Academy site.

Years in the planning, the new high school is long-awaited: "What's struck me is that everyone has been waiting such a long time for a new secondary school that doesn't involve tortuous travel arrangements. One pupil said to me: 'It'll be one short bus journey for me, but my older brother has to take two buses to his school now.' I expect many of our new pupils will be within walking distance or at least a short yellow bus ride away from the Academy." Guy Hutchence, Principal Designate.

"...it's been about designing a public sector building that is relevant and accessible to everyone. With the library and communal sports facilities, the Academy is going to be a huge resource right in the middle of this community."

Libby Graham, Director of Social Programmes.

Guy Hutchence, Councillor Sheila Newman (Manchester City Council's Executive Member for Children's Services) and pupils from local primary schools get their hands dirty!

1st April

Opening of the community orchard at Philips Park.

"We've had an orchard of one sort or another here for many years. The interest had waned until this year when Julie Lawrence and Ryan Tracey (I love 'em to bits) from the Environment Team stepped in and reinvigorated the orchard. This year alone we've had about 600 schoolchildren visit us, and they've loved every minute.

"The future for the orchard is fantastic. There are willing volunteers who'll maintain it all year round, in all weathers, and all we need is for the powers that be to help get people down here to admire it, acknowledge it and enjoy it."

Bill Booth, Clayton resident.

"Over the past ten years the housing market has been dramatically transformed. Thousands of ex-council houses have been renovated and hundreds of high quality new homes are now being occupied by both existing residents and those wanting to move to the new east Manchester."

Sean McGonigle.

4th April

Medlock Valley gets two regeneration awards.

The £2 million invested in the Medlock Valley since 2006 is well spent according to the British Urban Regeneration Association (BURA). The improvement project wins the Area Based Regeneration category and receives a commendation in the Community category at their Waterways Renaissance Awards.

20 09

30th April

Submission of NDC Succession Strategy outlining how the benefits of the NDC programme will be sustained through New East Manchester.

12th June

The New Roundhouse opens in Openshaw. It's home to Manchester Settlement who have moved from Beswick.

> "We run an education programme for young people between 13 and 16 who, for any number of reasons, aren't able to fulfil their full potential at mainstream secondary schools. Maybe they're facing challenging circumstances at home or have other issues which mean that the local high school isn't the best place for them to learn effectively."
>
> **Maria Gardner, General Manager, Manchester Settlement.**

2nd August

The sun shines on east Manchester's biggest annual event.

4,000 attend the 7th annual summer Parties in the Park event at Philips Park. As part of the event, the Seeds of the East festival offers a host of family friendly activities with a 'grow your own' theme including two gardening themed children's shows, craft workshops where kids make festival hats, decorate pots, build kites or recycle tin cans into clocks.

26th August

The Learning4U resource – information on local courses – goes online as a one-stop portal at www.L4Ueast.com.

7th September

Inaugural meeting of the Beacons Community Partnership.

"A lot of the existing community engagement framework comes from NDC. But now our funding is coming to an end, that framework will no longer exist. After we'd reviewed what residents wanted we suggested there should be three new groups to take the place of the Residents' Forum. So that's where these new Community Partnerships come in. They will still include residents' groups but now there's opportunity for wider input from faith groups, other interest groups and the voluntary sector. The Beacons Community Partnership, and the two others in Miles Platting & Newton Heath and Gorton, will make sure residents continue to input into the regeneration of their area. Each will also select a representative to sit on the New East Manchester Board."

Lesley Spencer, Principal Regeneration Officer.

"Everyone is a little bit worried about New Deal coming to an end but these community partnerships have got to be a good thing. It's the only way the community are going to stay involved. They are new at the moment, but in a few months, when they all come together for one big consultation, that's when we'll know if it's working."

Irene Baron, Clayton resident.

Compared to 2000 there's been a 46% reduction in burglary and a 58% reduction in vehicle crime this year.

Source: NDC administrative data from Social Disadvantage Research Centre, University of Oxford and 2008/9 GMP crime data.

September

After four months of dismantling, the ill-fated *B of the Bang* sculpture is finally brought to the ground, although its name lives on. 'B of the Blog' is a community media project run by People's Voice Media and 'Bang of the Voice' is the North East District Youth Forum.

21st September

The regeneration continues...

Plans for a £24 million BMX centre are approved. Designed by Ellis Williams Architects, the building will, with the existing Manchester Velodrome, form the National Cycling Centre, the British home of cycling. It will include a 2,000-seat BMX area and offices for the headquarters of the British Cycling Federation.

25th September

Topping out ceremony at the East Manchester Academy.

Local MP Tony Lloyd and Principal Designate Guy Hutchence are transported in a 'scissor lift' to make their marks on one of the highest steel beams. "I wrote 'Be the change you want to see', and Mr Lloyd wrote, 'Here our children's dreams come true.'"

Guy Hutchence.

28th September

Greggs officially open their new bakery in Openshaw.

This new £16 million state-of-the-art facility supplies 150 North West shops and employs 220 staff. But now they have the capacity for much more!

23rd October

NEM Staff Away Day.

Staff volunteers disperse around east Manchester doing good work.

One group head to Philips Park cemetery with residents and 'friends of the park' to plant bulbs, clean the memorials and clear the headstones.

23rd October

After 12 years working in east Manchester, Sean McGonigle moves on. His leaving 'do' is at the Grange in Beswick. Sean is promoted to Assistant Chief Executive at Manchester City Council.

"He's been with it right from the beginning... he's helped set the whole thing up. You knew where you were with Sean. He listened to everyone, and he would give his own opinion. He was always fair. I would like to think he would stay, but because he's successful at what he does, he'll have to move on."

Doreen Burns, Beswick resident.

"If they hadn't picked Sean, I don't know, I just don't know. I warmed to him very quickly, which I wasn't expecting at all."

Elaine Wright, Openshaw resident.

"I'll say one thing: I would never have been in this if Sean McGonigle hadn't been running things. I've got the greatest faith in him. I've fought rings around him, don't get me wrong, but he's been the one that's led us, and helped us all. If we had a problem, we'd go to Sean and it was fixed. We used to call him 'Father Sean' because we'd take all our problems to him. He's earned this promotion, he most certainly has. I'm going to his leaving do and I'll give him that fiver I owe him... in a frame!"

Maggie Warburton, Clayton resident.

Maggie Warburton presents Sean McGonigle with 'that fiver I owe him' (see page 11).

2009

23rd November

Start on site of £40 million Openshaw District Centre.

Luke Murphy and Kate Weir, both ten, from St Clement's C of E Primary School in Openshaw join representatives from the City Council, New East Manchester, Dransfield Properties and Morrisons (the 'anchor' tenant) to cut the first sod of turf.

November

Demolition begins of Rolls-Royce's Crossley Works on Pottery Lane.

10th December

EnterPrize All Stars event held at Gorton Monastery.

The winners of the £10,000 top prize are Wigs Up North, a make-up and wigs supplier for theatre and TV.

Jackie Sweeney, Vicky Holmes and Liz Armstrong from Wigs Up North

21st December

Succession strategy approved.

The Government approves the strategy detailing how the successes of the NDC programme are to be continued in the sustained regeneration of east Manchester.

26th March 2010

Celebration event at Gorton Monastery to mark the end of the Beacons programme and the tenth anniversary of New East Manchester.

The Last Word.

"Let me reassure anyone who needs to know: this has been the finest NDC in the land. You can like them or loath them, but we've had a very professional team doing a very hard job to the best of their ability. And how can you not be supportive of all this regeneration?

"Everything they've put in has been massively positive, and let's be thankful we're not left with any white elephants. Look at the velodrome – and all those gold medals we've just won – we're the envy of the world.

"But regeneration comes with a bad package as well, and that's housing. We're talking about people's lives, and whole communities. What do we do when residents don't agree with the regeneration bosses? There are no easy answers, but it needs serious thought."

Bill Booth, Clayton resident.

"I open my curtains now and I see hanging baskets, a lovely park, fantastic new front gardens, all the things they said we would have. If you pick up the phone for a repair – a grid overflowing or a street light – they're here the next day. And everyone is going round much more cheerfully. It amazes me. You look back and think what it was like. We were on the point of moving out. Our houses were worth nothing. We felt like prisoners in our own homes. You went in, locked your door, closed your curtains, that was it."

Wendy Eaton, Openshaw resident.

"At the start of all this I was driving a taxi. Now after doing courses, working first as a volunteer and then as an employee in youth work, I can look back proudly at everything I've achieved. I'm now the deputy manager at a children's centre elsewhere in the city."

Jeff Burns, Openshaw resident.

"Appointing local people was one of the best things they could have done. That works. Even with the best intentions, people coming in from the better parts of town do not understand what it's like to live in this area."

Dot Rathbone, Beswick resident.

"If I went back in time now, right to the start, and tried to do what is now accepted practice, the officers wouldn't be ready for it. The residents would... but not the officers."

Paul Cullen, former Community Safety Co-ordinator.

"If you close your eyes and imagine what the place was like 13 years ago and then look at it now... well, it's just incomparable. Everything from the stadium, Asda, the armadillo-shaped velodrome to the smallest back entry. At every level the area is physically a million per cent improved. Every corner looks different.

"So many phenomenal people have worked together to achieve this change. You could spend all day naming them, there have been so many. They have committed so much time and energy, so much of themselves."

Claire Evans, 4CT Chief Executive (former JOG Co-ordinator).

"Two of my children moved from Manchester because this area was so bad. They took seven grandchildren with them. I thought that was awful, they'd had to move because there was nothing for them here. I think that's been my biggest motivation for getting involved. I wanted to see a change and be part of that change, and it's been a unique experience..."

Linda Wagner, Beswick resident.

"We've learnt an awful lot. A lot of us were 'gobby' to start with but I do think working with The Establishment – whatever or whoever that is – has made us more confident. We've met a lot of people and we've had a lot of attention. I have no fear of talking to anyone, ministers or whoever, about our area and the success we've had with NDC.

"I do worry, though, about who's going to take it forward. We need some new blood, someone to challenge when things aren't right."

Barbara Taylor, Beswick resident.

"It used to be very depressing. I'd come in and out of our street blinkered, not looking at any of the houses. But, if you were to walk round now, it's changed a thousand per cent. All the ex-council stock have got their new windows and doors and look fabulous. The terraced houses have had a facelift: the privet hedges have come down and nice railings put up, and we've got new front gardens. That muddy square of grass has now got trees on it and boulders round. The field opposite – we had to fight for that – but that's now the Millennium Green with a play area and football pitch. There aren't any boarded-up houses any more, some have been demolished and converted into garden extensions... and there are bungalows for the elderly going up, which look fantastic."

Elaine Wright, Openshaw resident.

"New Deal has made my area friendly. They've made it liveable, and people are happier. We chose to stay and I'm glad we did. We could have upped and left but we decided to stick it out and see it through. I feel really quite passionate now about where we live. It's scary to think of what it could have been like now without all that money."

Andrea Melarkey, Clayton resident.

"It's the best job I've ever had. No two days have ever been the same. For me, working with such a long-established team – all of whom I have personally recruited – has made the work even more rewarding. We're totally focused on what we are doing and every single residents' success motivates us even further."

Carol Bartram, Head of Economic Development

"Looking back, it was a fantastic process and it gave us a lot of opportunities. Many local people have got jobs out of it and moved on to better things. I would love for it to go on for another ten years but that isn't going to happen. People are a bit scared it'll go back to the way it was, you know, when you didn't know what was going on and no-one told you anything."

Diane Vickers, Clayton resident.

"There is room for criticism, maybe we could have done more, but we need to remember just how much we have achieved in ten years. It feels like we've made more changes in the last ten years than were made in the preceding 30.

"What's significant is that we've had enough people in east Manchester who believed we could make a difference, and that together, we could make it happen.

"We have been at the forefront of changing mainstream public services in Manchester. The improvements in service delivery now are directly influenced by the work we've done in east Manchester."

Philip Bradley, Principal Regeneration Officer.

"Ten years have flown by. There have been significant physical changes but there are still areas that are not great and there is a lot still to do. But our communities have changed. By and large, we don't have the same community spirit as we used to. Just two generations ago, people lived and worked in the same area. Families grew up in the same streets as other families for generations, everyone knew everyone else, it was like a big village. I'm not saying it was Utopia and everyone was a wonderful neighbour, but at least you knew where you stood. It's a shame this spirit hasn't survived."

Irene Johnson, Beswick resident.

"Personally the high point was seeing individuals take the opportunity to send their life courses off in different directions. Yes, you can improve a park or build new houses – all of that is important – but seeing people make positive choices about changing their lives was, for me, massive. There were enough examples of that to know that we really did make a difference."

Tracey Annette, former Resident Liaison Officer.

"You can never attain 100% success. But with all this investment and the effort people have put in, I think they have done a bloody good job, I really do. Ten years is a short time in a regeneration process and there are benefits, in education, for example, that are still to be felt."

Hedley Carter, Chariot Office Supplies and Beacons Board Member.

"Yes, we've got CCTV, we've got wardens, we've got the police, we've got neighbour nuisance, we've got RSLs [Registered Social Landlords]. But we've still got crime in our area. It's a helluva lot better than it was, but there's still a lot to do."

Elaine Wright, Openshaw resident.

"Residents' expectations have increased because of NDC. Since the area has improved, people expect more... they deserve more. They won't tolerate what they did 10–15 years ago because they know it can be tackled at an earlier stage. They've seen what can be done, and now they tell us sooner if there are problems."

Jackie Hynes, Community Safety Manager, Eastlands Homes.

"It was a moment in time. For Groundwork it was six years of fantastic opportunity, driven by strong co-ordination and a clear vision."

Jason Brindle, Groundwork MSSTT.

"Without a doubt, the best thing to come out of all this has been the community involvement. Before 1999 you could never get an answer from the town hall, on anything. NDC has empowered the community as a whole to challenge the Council on the services they deliver, and that's worked very well."

Irene Baron, Clayton resident.

"It was an adventure. It changed people's lives. For me, it was fantastic working with, and learning from, residents. I'm very grateful and privileged to have done it. I'd be especially pleased if FC United gets a ground in east Manchester... that'd just top it!"

Paul Cullen, former Community Safety Co-ordinator.

"Already things aren't looking as sharp as they should be. It's only small things like graffiti on a park sign or a burnt-out bin, but after spending all that money it should still be tiptop. It was always acknowledged that the regeneration would continue, and I don't think anyone ever thought they'd do everything in ten years, did they?"

Tracey Annette, former Resident Liaison Officer.

"My view is that New Deal for Communities in east Manchester has been a huge success. Why do I say that? It has been at the forefront of a critical phase over the last ten years of transforming public services within the city. If you look at all the major developments in service delivery, almost exclusively they have started in the east and have been underpinned by New Deal for Communities. The most obvious one is neighbourhood policing... tried out here and then rolled out across the city and the rest of Greater Manchester. There have been advances in economic programmes, street environment management and neighbour services, all started here in the east.

"I'm optimistic for the future because these transformations have now been embedded into mainstream public services. Ten years on, public servants better understand residents' needs. I appreciate there are concerns about what happens beyond this successful New Deal programme, but local people now have a clear voice over the future of their streets, their neighbourhoods, and their communities and public services are now better equipped to respond more proactively to these challenges. That's a very powerful legacy to leave behind."

Eddie Smith, Chief Executive, New East Manchester.

"He'd have been two when it all started, and there was next to nothing here, really very little. But since the regeneration he's really benefitted. His primary school had an awful lot of money pumped in for computers and play facilities. Then there's been the community garden at home, and all his sporting things. He's done athletics, football, he's still doing the cycling at the velodrome, and then there's the trapeze course he did with his dad. How many 12-year-olds get the chance of doing a trapeze course?!"

Andrea Melarkey, Clayton resident.

"I think some of it's worked and some of it hasn't. Some things they've done are first class. I love my new house, it's lovely and really economical. But it's not buildings that regenerate an area, it's about homes, families and the roots you put down. Now we've got new houses and apartments, which are all very nice, but many are bought to let, so the new residents haven't any commitment to the area."

Josie Fletcher, Clayton resident.

> "We've achieved a lot and what we've learned has been used across the city. But there's no sitting back in this job: there are still some complex lives out there and changing them for the better takes time."
>
> **Libby Graham, Director of Social Programmes.**

"For me, New Deal has been the best thing that's happened to east Manchester... I don't want it to end! The place looks so much better, the nuisance neighbour situation has improved: New Deal has stepped in to point them in the right direction. But I am worried it might slip back... I hope it doesn't, but that does worry me."

June Webb, Beswick resident.

"How naive is this? We thought if we could get into schools, get to the kids before they were 11, that this next generation would be different. But they're not. In some cases, where drugs and drinking's concerned, they're worse. That's a disappointment, because I still see groups of youths on streets, wandering around, all day and all night. No jobs, no intentions of getting jobs."

Barbara Taylor, Beswick resident.

> "I think New Deal was a very brave experiment. There were some positive things to come from it that have now infected the way public services are delivered. I just hope that government can now take what we have learnt and develop more new models that will enable local people to really take hold of their own communities. I've learnt an enormous amount from NDC and I think that without it, there are some people who would not have gained the skills or confidence to transform their own lives."
>
> **Hilary Armstrong MP, Minister of State with responsibility for Local Government and Housing, 1997–2001.**

"I just want people to know how wonderful east Manchester is, because it is a wonderful place to live. The way people band together, the community spirit, you're definitely part of a big community now... and you feel wanted."

Wendy Eaton, Openshaw resident.

"Trust and honesty. That's what's needed. I've never known residents believe anyone before, but they did believe in Sean. And the people he brought in from other agencies... they didn't think themselves something they weren't. Everyone adapted straight away."

Elaine Wright, Openshaw resident.

"It's hard to appreciate just how far we have travelled over the last 11 years, a journey that has been as challenging as it has been exhilarating. Without doubt, it's been the most rewarding work I have ever been involved in and I have a huge admiration and respect for all those residents who have freely given up their time to help make a difference and make sure that, collectively, we got it right. I firmly believe we did!"

Sean McGonigle.

Acknowlegements

Len Grant would like to thank all the east Manchester residents and officers who have contributed to *Reclaiming East Manchester*. Lucy Banks' transcription skills have been indispensable in pulling hours and hours of interviews together. Thanks also to Sportcity Manager, Gary Crate and Radford Advertsing for providing historical information and images. Jeni Quirke, Roz Hughes and many others at New East Manchester have helped by supplying images, dates, statistics and advice. And to Lesley Spencer and Sean McGonigle for guiding the editorial process and Alan Ward for his graphic design.

About the author

Photographer and writer Len Grant has documented regeneration in Manchester for nearly 20 years. In his 2004 book, *Space to inspire*, commissioned by New Deal for Communities and Groundwork, he began recording east Manchester residents' experiences of regeneration, a process which is still ongoing. Between 2005–09 he and Alan Ward at Axis Graphic Design produced ten issues of the award-winning *East* magazine (see page 127) which continues online at www.thisiseast.com. In 2010 he will also publish a personal project about social exclusion entitled *Billy and Rolonde*.

Photographic credits

Anne Worthington was the first photographer to be commissioned by Beacons and her images of the early years and a dilapidated east Manchester appear on pages 6, 8, 17, 34-36, 40-42, 44, 45, 56, 58, 59, 66, 101 (bottom). Other credits include Della Batchelor: 48; Nathan Cox: 69, 76, 86 (top); Len Grant: 4, 30, 32, 61, 62, 64, 68, 70, 72, 75, 78 (right), 80, 81, 83-85, 88-89, 105, 108, 110, 116, 117, 119-128, 129 (bottom), 131 (background), 133 (below), 136-147, 149 (bottom), 151, 153, 155 (bottom), 156 (top), 158-160, 161 (bottom), 162, 163 (top), 164, 166 (middle), 167-170, 173, 174 (middle), 176 (middle), 183; Paul Herrmann: 33; Daniel Hopkinson: 171 (bottom); Manchester Library and Information Service: Manchester Archives and Local Studies: 20, 24-29; Karen Wright Photography: 131 (bottom), 163 (bottom), 166, 172, 174 (top), 176 (top, bottom). Also page 22, courtesy of The Co-operative Group. Apologies for uncredited images.

 NEWEASTMANCHESTER

Published in 2010 by Len Grant Photography on behalf of
New Deal for Communities and New East Manchester Ltd.
187 Grey Mare Lane
Beswick
Manchester
M11 3ND

ISBN-13: 978-0-9526720-6-7

Reclaiming East Manchester has been commissioned to celebrate the completion of the New Deal for Communities programme in east Manchester, 1999-2010.

Further copies can be purchased online at www.cornerhouse.org/books